DAWN'S EARLY LIGHT

—⁂—

By
Larry R. Haggard

Copyright © 2016 by Larry R. Haggard

Dawn's Early Light

by Larry R. Haggard

Printed in the United States of America

ISBN 978-1-940609-59-1

All rights reserved solely by the author. The author guarantees all contents are original and do not infringe upon the legal rights of any other person or work. No part of this book may be reproduced in any form without the permission of the author. The views expressed in this book are not necessarily those of the publisher.

Unless otherwise indicated, Bible quotations are taken from the King James Version of the Bible.

FWB Publications
Columbus, Ohio

DEDICATION

—⁂—

*This book is dedicated to my wife, Rose.
Since she did most of the work,
she deserves the credit.*

Table of Contents

1. The Early Light 9
2. The Christ Bearer 15
3. God or Gold 39
4. A Consuming Fire 45
5. The Protestant Wind 55
6. The Forbidden Book 67
7. God has a Plan 75
8. In the Name of God – Amen 87
9. A City Upon a Hill 111
10. Conceived in Liberty 123
11. The Most Misunderstood Man in America ... 131
12. The Rise of Other Colonies in America 143
13. The Salem Witch Trials 155
14. Missions in America 161
15. In Adam's Fall, We Sinned All 167
16. Wars and Rumors of Wars 177
17. Pilgrim's Progress 183
18. A Sleeping Giant 195
19. The Great Awakening 203
20. The War to Begin All Wars 217

21. The Battle Cry of Freedom 227
22. The Shot Heard Around the World................241
23. No King But King Jesus 251
24. In the Course of Human Events....................261
25. The Hand of God...279
26. The World Turned Upside Down 301

Endnotes..311
Bibliography 325

1

The Early Light

The cross of Christ is the focal point of all history. In fact, it has been stated that the study of mankind is "His story." The history of America is, in many ways, the study of the free and enslaved man. Throughout the ages, since the fall (Genesis 3:1-7), man has been a slave to sin. At Calvary, Christ died to set mankind free from the law of sin and death (Romans 8:2). The rough and rugged road to freedom thus begins at the foot of the cross.

The persecution of the New Testament church drove thousands of Jewish believers from their homeland in Israel to Europe, to seek the freedom to worship and serve God as the Creator dictated. In spite of the rebellion of Israel and the persecution of the church, God has always had a distinct plan for His people. For nearly one-third of a millennium, the early Christian believers had to withstand brutal persecution at the hands of Roman tyrants. In spite of this severe persecution, these bold followers of Jesus carried the gospel message to most of Europe.

The Roman emperor, Constantine, supposedly received a vision of a cross in the sky in A.D. 313. Believing this was a message from the Christian god, he repealed the prohibition against their religion and made Christianity the state religion of his empire. With the freedom to worship restored and the ability to live the Christian life, licensed Christianity should have flourished, but it did not. A corrupt Catholic church emerged by centralizing power in Rome. In time, the Pope would even exercise more power than the emperor. For a millennium, the power and the influence of the Roman church grew unchecked. It influenced every area of life; the sciences, literature, politics, and religion. Catholicism transcended governments and infiltrated into cultures and societies. The Pope and his church ruled with an iron fist and controlled most of Europe. By 1229, the church decreed that only the clergy could possess the Holy Scriptures. This practice helped remove any question of the church's authority over its congregants, but it also aided in propelling Europe into its Dark Ages. In the midst of the spiritual ignorance of the Middle Ages, the lamp of learning grew dim in almost every area of life.

> Without the light of God's Word to guide them, the people were led into the Dark Ages, a time of spiritual error and paganism. The mass replaced the Lord's Supper; church ritual supplanted salvation by grace. Sinful, human priests replaced Christ, the true believer's great High Priest and the only

Mediator between God and man. Purgatory took its supposed place beside Hell, so that the church could collect money from parishioners by offering a false hope that dead loved ones might be delivered from torment through financial sacrifices.

Worship became idolatrous; it was directed toward Mary and other saints, as well as toward human bones and other special relics, most of which were fraudulent. By the fourteenth century, the church even unofficially taught the infallibility of the pope's official statement, thereby giving the pope an attribute that only God possesses. Roman Catholicism became a religion based on ceremony and material 'charms'; it departed from true Christianity, which is based on spiritual redemption by personal faith in Christ.

One of the most repulsive practices of the Roman church was the selling of indulgences, which became widespread during the fifteenth and sixteenth centuries. The church taught that many of her saints had prayed and suffered more than was necessary for the individual salvation and had thereby created a reserve of forgiveness. This reserve was sold in the form of indulgences (although the church never admitted that indulgences were 'for sale' as such). If a person were sufficiently wealthy, he could even buy indulgences to take care of future sins, thus in effect obtaining advance permission to sin.[1]

God used the Renaissance and the Reformation to break the enslaving hold that the Catholic Church had upon Europe during the fifteenth and sixteenth centuries. The Renaissance was characterized by a rebirth of learning. Although most secular historians applaud the advancements in the arts and humanities during that time, God used the invention of the moveable type printing press and the mass production of the Scriptures that brought about the revival of the reading of God's Word and the Protestant Reformation.

The work and sacrifice of untold numbers of men and women of faith is what led to the exploration of the Americas. Men like John Wycliffe, who devoted his life to preserving the Scriptures, and Martin Luther, who set his life and work aside to stand upon the truths of justification by faith and opposed the heresy of the Catholic church, were instrumental in church reform. The Swiss reformers, Zwingli and Calvin, helped bring their nations out of the Dark Ages to enlightenment and advancement in almost every area of life. Meno Simons, an Anabaptist preacher from Holland, gathered groups of dissenters and organized them into churches that became the Mennonite and Baptist pioneers in the New World. This hallowed company included the martyrs of European religious persecution, who would contribute to the cause of Protestantism with their lives' work as well as their lives.

We cannot understand the founding of America without understanding the reformation in Europe. There is evidence to believe that America was explored by Europeans many times prior to Columbus. There are Irish, Celtic, Scandinavian and Jewish legends that speak of the "New World," some as early as 2000 B.C. Interesting evidence dots the American landscape that points to pre-Columbian exploration by Europeans. This is a testimony to their adventuresome spirit and rugged constitution, but not to their desire to extend their level of civilization to the other side of the globe. It is obvious that these people had no motivation to settle or exploit their finds, and they left no written word of their explorations. It was not until the Protestant Reformation and the intense persecution of the Inquisition that Europeans began to look to the Western Hemisphere for serious exploration. The intense persecution of the Catholic Church, linked with the intense desire to evangelize the world, propelled Europeans to new lands. It is true that many explorers and their financiers sought for gold in the New World, but it is equally true that many sought God and His new "Promised Land."

2

The Christ Bearer

It is believed that Christopher Columbus, or Columbo, as it is written in Italian, was born in Genoa, Italy in 1435. However, no one is sure of his exact date or place of birth. Precious little is known about the man who is hailed to be the discoverer of the Americas. Mystery surrounds him from cradle to grave. His life appears to be shrouded, either by his own design or by schemes of the people or peoples who wished to capitalize on his fame and discoveries. After half a millennium, the world still wonders who this aspiring mariner was. Several nations claim him. Even more amazing is that several religions hail him as one of theirs. Even his writings leave the reader in a quandary over his motives and means of exploring the New World.

The traditional accounts of Columbus state that he was the eldest of four children born to Dominico Columbo and his wife, Susannah Fonatanarossa of Genoa. Young Christopher apparently rejected his father's trade of woolcombing early in life. For a brief time, he was sent to the University of Pavia, where he studied geography, astronomy, mathematics, and navigation.

His life at sea began in his early teens. The Spanish historian, del Almirante, pinpoints the age at fourteen years, but others claim he was still in Genoa for several more years. Washington Irving notes that the youthful Italian adventurer made the maiden voyages alongside a distant, unnamed relative, "a veteran of the seas, who had risen to some distinction by his bravery, and is occasionally mentioned in old chronicles, sometimes as commanding a squadron of his own, sometimes as an admiral in the Genoese service."[1]

A seaman's life on the Mediterranean in the fifteenth century was a daring one. Stormy seas were compounded by tempestuous times: insidious acts of piracy, naval and military graft and corruption, and frequent feuds between the divided Italian states. It was during these times that Columbus began his illustrious nautical career. From those early days, when the young Genoan was a wide-eyed adventurer, to his autumn years, when the hearty veteran of the seas writes of his exploits, two facts remain the same: his faith and confidence in himself and his faith in his Creator.

Columbus possessed a strong natural genius, but he viewed this as a God-given virtue. He put his thirst for knowledge and hunger for adventure to good use by studying and learning from the best of his time. He learned the art of mapmaking from the Portuguese, the premier cartographers of the day. He also developed his paradigm of the earth from the exploits of Prince Henry, the great Portuguese navigator. It was Henry's idea to circumnavigate Africa, thereby opening a quicker trade route to Asian markets, but in the 1400s, navigation on the open Atlantic was in its infancy. Henry founded a naval college and observatory to bring together the most learned of Europe. The results were phenomenal. At once, the tiny country of Portugal began to excel in cartography and naval exploration. The use of new technology, such as the compass, was also brought into common use. By the end of Henry's life in 1473, Portugal had risen from a small, insignificant country in southwestern Europe to a world power that, for a brief moment, ruled the seas. It was at this moment that Columbus was thrust upon the scene of world events.

Not long after his arrival in Lisbon, the pious Columbus met Dona Telepa Perestrello, the daughter of Prince Henry's distinguished navigator, at religious services of the All Saints Chapel. They married, and the young couple took up residence in the Portuguese capitol. Columbus supported his family by sailing and mapping navigational maps, but longed for more – to explore the unknown. His theories of the unknown were firmly based upon that which he did comprehend. Even though some theologians and cartographers held to the belief of a flat Earth, Columbus and others embraced the doctrine of a spherical Earth. This view was firmly based upon the Scriptures that refer to the "circle of the earth" in Isaiah 40:22. Columbus also viewed his role in seeking a western route to India as a God-advanced mandate.

When Columbus had formed his theory, it became fixed in his mind with singular firmness, and influenced his entire character and conduct. He never spoke in doubt or hesitation, but with as much certainty as if his eyes had beheld the promised land. No trial nor disappointment could divert him from the steady pursuit of his object. A deep religious sentiment mingled with his meditations, and gave them at times a tinge of superstition, but it was of a sublime and lofty kind; he looked upon himself as standing in the hand of Heaven, chosen from among men for the accomplishment of its high purpose; he read, as he supposed, his contemplated discovery foretold in Holy Writ, and shadowed forth darkly in the mystic revelations of the prophets. The ends of the earth were to be brought together, and all nations and tongues and languages united under the banners of the Redeemer. This was to be the triumphant consummation of his enterprise, bringing the remote and unknown regions of the earth into communion with Christian Europe; carrying the light of the true faith into benighted and Pagan lands, and gathering their countless nations under the holy dominion of the Church.[2]

With God's leadership, the Genoan visionary boldly presented the plan to the attentive king of Portugal, John II. If the monarch would supply and fit seaworthy ships, Columbus would sail west, across the treacherous Atlantic, claim any islands that he discovered for Portugal, and reach India from the east. Historians disagree as to why Columbus's proposal was rejected. However, most agree that he was bold, self-confident and even overbearing in his demand for recognition of his exploits. Columbus broke off all negotiations with Portugal when he realized that King John had sent a ship to determine the validity of such a mission. The trusting mariner had supplied the king with a detailed map and plan for his voyage. Secretly, John sent explorers west using Columbus's own plan. These weary mariners aborted the plan on the stormy Atlantic and fearfully returned to the safety of Portugal after only several days on the open seas.

Columbus, having lost his wife, and now his vision for extending the supremacy of her native Portugal on the seas of the Atlantic, secretly departed for his native land on the Italian peninsula. While in Genoa, the energetic Columbus submitted his exploration proposal to the Genoan government, but by 1484, the tiny Italian republic was nearing its demise and had no energy or resources to aid her native son.

It was at this time that Columbus convinced his brother, Bartholomew, to extend his proposal to the king of England. Once again, he was rejected, or for a better word, ignored. It is also speculated that the optimistic Columbus made a presentation to the Venetians concerning his venture of establishing a western trade route to India. Even though there is no documentation of this offer, the reply is obvious and the adventurer peddled his plans elsewhere.

France was to be the next target for the weary Columbus. Since God had ordained his enterprise, he needed only to find a wealthy financier to endorse the cause and Columbus would be on his way. Before the adventurous Columbus could approach the French crown, the wealthy Duke of Medina convinced him to petition the monarchs of Spain. The marriage of Ferdinand and Isabella had consolidated the Catholic powers of the Iberian Peninsula. This mighty alliance had put an end to the nation's internal strife and was about to vanquish the Moorish control of the country. It was during the Spanish conquest of the dreaded Moors that Columbus had his first audience with King Ferdinand.

> Ferdinand was too keen a judge of men not to appreciate the character of Columbus. He perceived that, however soaring might be his imagination, and vast and visionary his views, his scheme had scientific and practical foundation. His ambition was excited by the possibility of discoveries far more important than those which had shed such glory upon Portugal; and perhaps it was not the least recommendation of the enterprise to this subtle and grasping monarch, that, if successful, it would enable him to forestall that rival nation in the fruits of their long and arduous struggle, and by opening a direct course to India across the ocean, to

bear off from them the monopoly of oriental commerce.[3]

The wary king, though impressed by Columbus, deferred to advisors in the areas of science and religion before he gave the explorer his royal decision. Fernando de Talavera, confessor of the queen, was commissioned to assemble the most learned astronomers, cosmographers, and theologians for the purpose of examining the theories of Columbus. They in turn would report to the sovereign their findings and professional opinions. The royal council assembled at St. Stephen's convent in Salamaea, in 1486, to examine the Genoan in the areas of mathematics, geography, astronomy and, to be sure, theology. The theological debate reigned longest and loudest in the halls of St. Stephen's. The text of Scripture and the opinions of church fathers were cited at every possible occasion. Scripture was misapplied and church tradition superceded mathematical and scientific fact. For example, Washington Irving cites Psalm 104:3, Psalm 103 and a passage in Hebrews as proof texts that were used to prove that the earth was flat. None of these attest to a flat earth or destroy a spherical theory of the planet. Contrary to what most Americans believe, the Flat Earth Theory was the minority view in the fifteenth century. Columbus was simply basing his assumption on the theory of Ptolemy, the Alexandrian astronomer of the second century.

The Salamaean council met sporadically for months. In the spring of 1487, they adjourned to Cordova to fight the Moors. Columbus took up arms in this military campaign that lasted nearly half a year. Over the course of the winter, Columbus became disillusioned with the Spanish counsel and sent letters of inquiry to the English and Portuguese monarchs concerning resuming negotiations for the expedition to India. Apparently, when Ferdinand learned of this correspondence, he summoned the Italian to his court at Seville in 1489, but before the council could convene, the king was off to engage the Moors once again. Columbus quickly followed, and once again proved his valor on the field of battle. Finally in 1490, the impatient Columbus received his long-awaited answer from the Spanish sovereign.

> Fernando de Talavera, therefore, was commanded to inform Columbus, who was still at Cordova, that the great cares and expenses of the wars rendered it impossible for the sovereigns to engage in any new enterprise; but that when the war was concluded they would have both time and inclination to treat with him about what he proposed.

> Columbus was unwilling to receive it at second hand, and repaired to the court at Seville to learn his fate from the lips of the sovereigns. Their reply was virtually the same, declining to engage in the enterprise for the present, but holding out hopes of patronage when relieved from the care and expenses of the war.

Renouncing all further confidence, therefore, in vague promises, which had so often led to disappointment, and giving up all hopes of countenance from the throne, he turned his back upon Seville, indignant at the thoughts of having been beguiled out of so many precious years of waning existence.[4]

Reluctantly, Columbus once again began to look elsewhere for a sponsor for his venture. He set out on foot with his young son on a trek to France to engage the king. In the little seaport town of Palos de Moguier, the two weary travelers stopped at a convent to beg for bread and water. At this point, the course of world events changed drastically. Friar Juan Perez de Marchena, by chance, engaged the travelers in conversation. Since the area was a port, the topic of sea travel came up. The friar was amazed at the knowledge of the foreigner. So intrigued was he, that he begged Columbus to stay at the convent. The Pinzon brothers, local seamen, were invited to visit with the friar and his party. Martin Pinzon was so amazed with the natural genius and wealth of knowledge of this noted stranger that he committed his financial backing and ships to the Italian navigator if he could secure an endorsement from the Spanish crown for the expedition. Friar Perez, who was acquainted with Queen Isabella, dispatched a letter to the sovereigns, informing them that Columbus had the support of the most trusted maritime community in Spain. The trusted friar was summoned to Isabella, where he personally pled the case for Columbus. She called for Columbus to personally present himself at her court and sent 20,000 maravedis to pay for his transportation and wardrobe. From a chance refreshment stop at a lowly convent, Columbus received an audience with the queen. Fortunes had changed from France, back again to Spain.

The world took little notice of the threadbare Lombard in the winter of 1491. The eyes of Europe were focused upon King Ferdinand, who had finally vanquished the Moors. For nearly 800 years, the Muslims and Christians had struggled on the Iberian Peninsula. Now Columbus, a foreigner, was present to witness the Moorish final surrender. The day for which Spaniards had often besought Heaven had arrived; so too, Christopher Columbus had finally arrived.

> Their Catholic Majesties listened attentively to Columbus. And as it turned out, there had never been a time when they could have been any more receptive to his proposals. God had granted them a tremendous victory, and they had not thought of how they might show the heavenly Father their gratitude-build a cathedral, make a pilgrimage, erect shelters for the poor ... And now a far more modest possibility presented itself. Here, back again, was the Genoese visionary, with this proposal for his own Crusade: to discover new lands for the glory of God and His Church, and to spread the Gospel of the Holy Saviour to the ends of the earth.[5]

The royal negotiations with Columbus were directed through Fernando de Talavera, the archbishop of Grenada. From the onset, Columbus pridefully demanded royal titles and lavish reward for his exploits. De Talavera considered the pompous adventurer as merely a dreaming speculator unworthy of any demand upon the royals. Still, Columbus insisted and risked his mission with selfish demands, even though he had been pursuing the favor of the king, any king, for nearly eighteen years. As he considered appealing to France once again, Luis de St. Angel appealed to Isabella on his behalf.

He reminded her how much might be done for the glory of God, the exaltation of the Church, and the extension of her own power and dominion. What cause of regret to herself, of triumph to her enemies, of sorrow to her friends, should this enterprise, thus rejected by her, be accomplished by some other power! He reminded her what fame and dominion other princes had acquired by their discoveries; here was an opportunity to surpass them all. He entreated her majesty not to be misled by the assertions of learned men, that the project was the dream of a visionary. He vindicated the judgment of Columbus, and the soundness and practicability of his plans. Neither would even his failure reflect disgrace upon the crown. It was worth the trouble and expense to clear up even a doubt upon a matter of such importance, for it belonged to enlightened and magnanimous princes to investigate questions of the kind, and to explore the wonders and secrets of the universe. He stated the liberal offer of Columbus to bear an eighth of the expense, and informed her that all the requisites for this great enterprise consisted but of two vessels and about three thousand crowns.[6]

April 17, 1492 marked the end of Columbus's trek across Europe to secure royal endorsement and financial backing for his expedition. It also marked the beginning of his noble adventures into the regions beyond. The commission that was granted Columbus reflects his prideful demands:

1. He was granted the office of admiral in all the lands and seas that he discovered.
2. He would be the viceroy and governor-general over all lands that he claimed for Spain.
3. He could reserve one-tenth of the spoils of the expedition.
4. He or his subordinate would be the sole judge in all causes and disputes arising out of the traffic between the explored countries and Spain.
5. He would contribute one-eighth of the cost of the expedition and receive the same in profit from the expedition.

Since the nomadic Columbus had no bank account of his own, and barely was able to support himself with his trade of mapmaking, it is speculated that the finances which he pledged to the crown for one-eighth of the expense of the voyage must have been from the Pinzon brothers of Palos, or wealthy Jewish bankers. Legend insists that Queen Isabella pawned her royal jewels to finance this grand adventure. However, this is far from true. The monarchs charged Luis de Santangel, the keeper of the privy purse, to borrow the money from a security trust and a small portion from the royal treasury to finance their part of the venture.[7]

On the morning of August 3, 1492, Columbus took communion along with his men. They weighed anchor and set sail for India. The experienced cartographer and salty mariner never reached his goal. The ambitious visionary never realized his dreams of fame or fortune. He did sail west to follow his God-ordained course in life. The three ships reached the Canary Islands in less than a week of easy sailing. Columbus noticed that by using the prevailing winds, which were different on each side of the Tropic of Cancer, sail was made easier. He regarded these winds as provided by God, and thanked the Creator for the use of them.

Once on the open sea, the explorer realized his greatest danger was not the elements or even his ships. It was his crew. Most of the seasoned sailors were over ten times further out to sea than they had ever been. The vast expanse and the unknown of the Atlantic were overwhelming to them. Even the veteran Pinzon brothers, who captained two of the vessels, had seen enough. Finally, 3,000 miles from native Spain, Columbus agreed to abandon his dream if land was not sighted in three days. Had God allowed His faithful servant to suffer for 18 years only to face defeat and possibly death on the open seas? Facing mutiny, the Genoan navigator trusted God and held his course westward, hoping for a miracle.

At 2:00 a.m. on October 12, 1492, with less than four hours remaining before dawn of the third and final day, shouts rang out on the *Pinta*; land was sighted! Upon reaching shore, Columbus christened the island San Salvador, Holy Saviour in English, and prayed.

> "O Lord, Almighty and everlasting God, by Thy holy Word Thou has created the heaven, and the earth, and the sea; blessed and glorified be Thy Name, and praised be Thy Majesty, which hath deigned to use us, Thy humble servants, that Thy holy Name may be proclaimed in this second part of the earth.'[8]

In the next few weeks, Columbus hopped from one Caribbean island to the next, exploring and exploiting their bountiful supply. At this point, historians once again disagree as to the behavior of the Spaniards and their leader. Washington Irving continuously alludes to the fairness and compassion of Columbus, while Marshall and Manuel cite his cruel and careless manner with the natives. Either prospect leaves the motives of Columbus at question. While historians differ on treatment and motive, it seems evident that at all times, the Spanish eyes were searching for precious metals and stones. They secured interpreters from several islands to guide them to the supposed cache of gold on the next island. Several accounts carefully note natives wore golden jewelry. Columbus painstakingly notes landmarks, vegetation, animal life and the naked natives; but in the greatest detail, he specifies the gold in objects for which he traded.

Near midnight on Christmas Eve, Columbus's flag ship, the *Santa Maria*, ran aground and partially sank. The crew survived the ordeal and was quickly taken in by the Indians. Columbus decided to leave a company of 39 men to construct a fort, trade with the natives, and search for the source of their gold. As he departed, the governor general commanded his garrison to treat the Indians with dignity and respect. He assured them he would return for them at the first possible opportunity. Then, acting as admiral of the seas, he gave thanks to the God of Providence and set sail for the Spanish homeland.

The seas were calm, skies sunny, and with a steady tail of wind, the *Nina* and *Pinta* carried the adventurous heroes toward home, where they hoped to receive a much-deserved and long-anticipated, triumphant welcome. God had truly blessed them. Then on February 12, the seasoned mariners' nightmare was realized in a monstrous storm that threatened to swamp the small crafts. Miraculously, after days of torrential rain and ferocious winds, the storm subsided. The crew had begged God on the open sea for their lives. Once in port at the Portuguese Azores, they honored Him for His faithfulness.

It was here at Santa Maria Island that Columbus learned of a Portuguese plot to detain him and his ships while King John could send out his own expedition from Lisbon to claim the Spanish discoveries for Portugal. The wary Columbus slipped out of the Azorian port and set sail for Spain. Once again, a merciless winter storm struck the tiny *Nina*. For six days, the weary crew battled the raging storm. When land was finally sighted, the winds had delivered the Spanish admiral into the hands of the Portuguese King John. Columbus narrowly averted being ship-wrecked on the rocky crags of the Portuguese seashore by sailing into the River of Lisbon. Although Columbus's journal noted 25 ships had gone down on the same coast that winter, God graciously allowed him a free port.

Once on land, the quick thinking admiral sent word to King Ferdinand of his exploits. He then had an audience with King John in Lisbon. The Portuguese sovereign was gracious to his Spanish guest, offering to supply the explorer's every need, even to transport him by land to Spain. Columbus spent several days in the Portugal safe port, then departed for Spain when the weather permitted. On the 15th of March, Columbus, on board the *Nina*, sailed back to the home port of Palos, from which he departed on August 3 the previous year.

God's hand of providence had been upon Columbus, the Admiral of the Seas. He had endured years of ridicule, mockery and rejection. He had risked his life on the open seas, oftentimes against the odds, the elements and even his crew. Now his greatest enemy was before him. How would he react to success? Could Columbus enjoy the success and give God the credit and honor? Bjorn Lunstrom gives the following account:

> The Portuguese chroniclers write that the Admiral was so boastful and supercilious, saying that it was the King's fault for having rejected his proposals in the first place, that the courtiers, when they saw the Admiral so insolent and the King so unhappy, offered to kill Columbus and prevent his taking the news to Castile. But the King would not agree to that.[9]

Before the voyage of discovery, the visionary Columbus had been a humble beggar at the royal courts of Europe. Upon his return, he was an arrogant expeditionary with the world at his feet. He returned to Spain to a victor's welcome with festivals and parades. Ferdinand and Isabella immediately commissioned another voyage which Columbus would outfit and lead.

The lesson that one must learn is that God uses man even though he has imperfections. How God could use the prideful Columbus is amazing. In spite of his arrogance, the elevated Admiral of the Seas seems to have an immense faith in the Creator of the universe. Possibly it is that self-assurance that motivated Columbus to do what no other could, and to believe God had ordained him for the task.

Once back in Spain, the admiral was received by Ferdinand and Isabella as a conqueror returning from war, and justifiably so. Columbus had battled the elements, a shipwreck, several storms, and the challenges of a new hemisphere, and returned to testify of his exploits. He had conquered the seas, another world and the unknown. He was truly Admiral of the Seas. His reputation and accomplishments soon swept across Europe. In response to hearing of the Columbian discoveries, England's Henry VII pronounced the feat "a thing more divine than human." [10] Italians, especially the residents of Genoa, took great delight in their nation being the birthplace of the discoverer. Pope Alexander VI quickly responded to Columbus's discovery by issuing a Papal Bull and etching a line of demarcation on the globe from the north to south pole 100 leagues west of the Azores. This would protect the Portuguese holdings in the Atlantic Islands and on the African coasts, while allowing Spain to develop newly discovered lands in the western Atlantic.

Even though Columbus did not discover a water route to the Indies, or bring back large quantities of gold, his expedition was considered a success by Ferdinand and Isabella. Author John Boyd Thacker specifies the cost of the voyage in his 1902 book *Christopher Columbus*. His figures and their 2005 dollar equivalents are given below.

	1492	2005	
	Maravedis	Dollars	
Salary of Officers	268,000	$49,164	
Wages of Sailors	252,000	46,228	
Maintenance	319,680	58,644	
Rental Cost, Santa Maria	172,800	31,700	
Furnishings, Arms, Trading Supplies	155,062	28,446	
Total Expense	1,167,542	$214,182	[11]

The total cost of the venture compares to the one million maravedis salary of the Spanish Treasurer of State in 1492. The Spanish return on their investment, through the exploitation of riches from the New World, is estimated to be 200 million percent.

Columbus immediately began to plan a second voyage to expand his exploits and extend the influence of Christianity. His later writings uncover his burden to carry the gospel to the regions beyond.

"And your Highnesses, as Catholic Christians and Princes, devoted to the holy Christian faith and the propagation thereof-and enemies of the sect of Mohammet and of all idolatries and heresies, resolved to send me, Christopher Columbus, to the said regions of India, to see the said Princes and peoples and lands and the disposition of them and of all and the manner which may be undertaken their conversion to our holy faith. I prayed to the most merciful Lord about my heart's great desire, and He gave me that spirit and the intelligence for the task ... It was the Lord who put into my mind (I could feel His hand upon me) to sail to the Indies. All who heard of my project rejected it with laughter, ridiculing me. There is no question that the inspiration was from the Holy Spirit, because He comforted me with rays of marvelous illumination from the Holy Scriptures... encouraging me continually to press forward, and without ceasing for a moment they now encourage me to make haste. Our Lord Jesus desired to perform a very obvious miracle in the voyage to the Indies, to comfort me and the whole people of God. I spent seven years in the royal court...and in the end I, in order that they might develop a very friendly disposition toward us, because I knew that they were a people who could better be freed and converted to our holy faith by love than by force, gave to some of them the red caps and to others glass beads, which they hung on their necks and many other things of slight value, in which they took much pleasure...At this, they were greatly pleased and became so entirely our friends that it was a wonder to see... I believe that they would easily be made Christians, for it seemed to me that they had no religion of their own."[12]

But his actions as governor of Espanola portray him as a cruel tyrant who treated the Indians with contempt. So brutal was his treatment of the natives, Ferdinand and Isabella had him removed in irons from the island and returned to Spain. The proud admiral was eventually given his ships back, but never allowed to return to Espanola.

In subsequent voyages, he sailed to the New World, which he believed until his dying day was India. He did discover sizeable amounts of gold while exploring the Caribbean. This proved to be a curse more than a blessing, due to the Spanish explorers' cruel treatment of the natives of both North and South America. The conquistadors that followed Columbus imitated his barbaric behavior towards the Indians. The heritage of the Spaniards was far from being Christian; it was one of pillage, rape and murder.

Columbus spent the last part of his life writing of his travels and compiling commentaries of the Old Testament. He breathed his last breath on Ascension Day in 1506, with a prayer on his lips, "Father, into Thy hands I commend my spirit." In death, he was a broken man. He sailed west to find the Orient but never realized his goal, for he discovered a new world instead. He lusted for prestige, fame and fortune. These all were only temporal accolades for the Admiral of the Seas, who died a pauper, destitute of the king's finances or favor. He lived to see the liberation of the Holy Lands, only to die never realizing his dream or fulfilling his purpose. Could it have been God's will for Christopher, which means "Christ-bearer," to liberate the heathen in America instead of the Holy Land in Jerusalem? In reality, Columbus was the first to plant the cross of Christianity in the Western Hemisphere, but who was this man that brought Christ to the New World?

> Much has been written about the motives that prompted Columbus to risk his life and future in an attempt to discover a westward route to the Orient. It is difficult, if not impossible, to know Columbus' true motives. Some Jewish historians believe that Columbus, like his financiers, was seeking a refuge for exiled Jews; some Protestant historians believe that he wanted to take the Protestant gospel to the Orient; and some Catholic historians portray him as a devout Catholic. Those less religiously inclined suggest that he was seeking wealth and fame. In any case, Columbus' *Book of Prophecies* makes it clear that he was a devout student of the Bible.[13]

Most historians place Columbus in one of three religious categories: Catholic, Christian or a converted Jew. Those who label Columbus a Catholic usually acknowledge his allegiance to Rome and claim he was devout in his Catholicism, which was his Christianity. Some Protestant historians hail him as very un-Catholic. After all, he read and quoted Scripture in a time when the church frowned on such or even worse. The old seaman, not a priest, even wrote commentaries on Scripture. Others even point to his Italian birth and a Jewish connection and believe that Columbus was a converted Jew and not a Catholic at all. In fact, he led his band of Jews in three tiny ships in 1492, to avoid Catholic persecution. In reality, Columbus may have been all three. He may have been born Jewish and truly converted to Christianity. For years, Christians have argued over which brand of Christian he was. Unfortunately, in the last half of the fifteenth century, the church that we know the most about was from Rome, and the Christianity we read of was Catholic. Was Columbus a Catholic? Probably so. His own writings testify of this. Was Columbus a Christian? Possibly so. His desire was to carry the gospel to new worlds. The answer to the discoverer's true relationship with Christ must be understood in light of the age in which he lived. In 1229, the Catholic Church decreed that only the clergy could possess Scripture. The Protestant Reformation was born a decade and a half after Columbus's death. The adventurous Genoan had little "light" from which to navigate through life. He did have the light of Scripture. This is evident in his personal testimony recorded in his journal.

> "I am a most unworthy sinner, but I have cried out to the Lord for grace and mercy

and they have covered me completely. I have found the sweetest consolation since I made it my whole purpose to enjoy His marvelous presence. No one should fear to undertake any task in the name of our Savior, if it is just and if the intention is purely for His holy service. The working out of all things has been assigned to each person by our Lord, but it all happens according to His sovereign will, even though He gives advice."[14]

How could he understand a forbidden book (the Bible) without knowing its author? How could he chart a course for a new world without the moral compass of God's Word and God's spirit? Void of the light of the Protestant Reformation and bound in the darkness of the Spanish Inquisition, Columbus undoubtedly was a communicant in the Catholic Church. He received the sacraments just prior to his death.[15] But, he appears to have walked in the light which he had. Only eternity will reveal his true relationship to the Christ for whom he was named.

3

God or Gold

In his journal, Columbus carefully and prayerfully stated his purpose for exploration. The extension of the gospel of Jesus Christ was apparently his overriding purpose and desire. Those who followed Columbus, however, forever changed and tainted his legacy of bearing Christ to the regions beyond the Atlantic.

Taking the same westward route as Columbus did, the Spaniard Ferdinand Magellan set sail for the Indies in 1519. He kept bearing south in an attempt to avoid the land mass that he believed kept him from his goal. This land, which Columbus believed to be India, was in reality a new hemisphere. Twenty years earlier, Amerigo Vespucci had declared the Columbian discovery a new continent, unexplored western lands, not the eastern extremities of civilization of which Marco Polo wrote. As Magellan sailed southward, he was amazed at the immense size of the continent. He sailed around the southern tip of South America into the Pacific Ocean. His weary, hungry seamen made their way to the Philippine Island, where they landed for provisions. The seafaring Spanish found themselves in a tribal war in their Pacific paradise. The deadly native dispute cost Magellan his life and almost ended the expedition. Only one of the Spanish ships escaped the island, to return to Europe in 1522 with 18 of the original 200 crewmen.

Although the brave Magellan, like Columbus, never realized his goal, his eighteen-member crew did circumnavigate the globe. This proved the Scriptural assertion of "the circle of the Earth" mentioned in Isaiah 40:22. No longer was the planet thought to be flat. The theory of a globe was proven and the fear of sailing off the map was forever removed. Though the belief of Columbus and many other trusted navigators, scientists and theologians was substantiated, their calculations as to the size of the earth were found to be in grave error. The sphere was much larger than anyone had calculated. Magellan's voyage demonstrated that a westward route was not practical unless a navigable passage could be found through the western land expanses.

The Spanish goal of reaching the Orient was soon supplanted by a desire to exploit their new discoveries in the Americas. In 1519, Hernando Cortes landed in Mexico to explore the interior of the continent. The European explorers were amazed upon discovering the highly developed Aztec civilization of central Mexico. These Native Americans had constructed worship centers that would rival the accomplishments of Egypt and Babylonia. Their architectural feats amazed the Spanish, but their religious beliefs and practices horrified them. Pagan practices of human sacrifice and the public display of these rituals prompted Cortes to conquer the Aztecs. But was his motive religion or riches? "Thus a military conqueror replaced a military dictator, and pagan Catholicism replaced the Aztec's pagan practices."[1]

Prompted by the discoveries of gold in the New World, men began to intensely explore their claims in America. In 1513, Juan Ponce de Leon sighted the mainland of Florida. He would return to this American southernmost peninsula eight years later to establish a crown colony and search for the ever-elusive Fountain of Youth. In 1519, Alverez Pineda explored much of the Atlantic coast of America. Two years later, Franscisco de Gordillo covered the same area, and in 1524, Esteban Gomez sailed the entire eastern seaboard from Nova Scotia to Florida. The Spanish launched an ill-fated expedition to the area which would become the Carolinas in 1526. The colonists were led by Lucas Vasquez Ayllon, who perished along with nearly three-fourths of the party in the cold, cruel American frontier.

> The Spanish Crown grants Lucas Vasquez de Ayllon a patent to colonize Florida and he sails from Hispaniola with 500 prospective colonists for the Cape Fear area of North Carolina. He tries to establish a settlement there near the Pedee River. During the fall and severe winter Ayllon and 350 others die. The survivors give up and return to Hispaniola.[2]

Hernando de Soto left the island of Cuba in 1539 to search for gold in the Mississippi Valley region. He discovered the inland water passage to the heartland of the continent, but he found no trace of the precious metals for which he sought. Francisco de Coronado was the next Spaniard to experience "Gold fever" and chase the fabled "Seven Cities of Gold." He fruitlessly searched the barren southwestern regions of North America, chasing one Indian tale after another. His 4,000-mile expedition took two years, but yielded no appreciable discoveries of the gold for which they so longed. Still, the Spanish pushed on into the interior of both North and South America. They established a few colonies in the north, but their focus became Mexico and South America, due to the discovery of vast supplies of precious metals there. But, along with these discoveries came the exploitation of the native peoples. Even during the governorship of Christopher Columbus, the Spanish cruelly abused the natives.

> Since violence, provocation and injustice from the Christians never ceased, some fled to the mountains, and others began to slay Christians, in return for all the wrongs and the torture they had suffered. When that happened, vengeance was immediately taken; the Christians called it punishment, yet not the guilty alone, but all who lived in a village or a district, were sentenced to execution or torture.

In two years, 100 thousand of the approximate native population of 300 thousand on Espanola had died or been killed! According to a count made eight years later, that figure had more than doubled, and four years after that there were only twenty thousand left alive. The nightmare holocaust went on; there was no waking up from it.[3]

This same treatment continued on the continent in Mexico and South America. Wherever the Spanish landed, they brought their lust for wealth and their mandate to extend Christianity, the universal brand, to every possible nation and people. The price was unbelievable. By force and by fear, the Spanish conquered the natives of America. What was the legacy of these Catholic conquistadors? It was one of rape, pillage and theft, all in the name of the heavy hand of the church. One might ask, "Where is God?" in those dark days of European conquest in the Americas. Though the Master of the Universe may not have been obligated to answer the prayers of the Incas or the Aztecs as they cried to any god that could deliver them from the sword or shot of the Spanish, He did have a plan for America and He was meticulously moving to perform His sovereign will, first in the Old World, and then in the new.

4

A Consuming Fire

The roots of American civilization come from all parts of the world, especially Europe. To understand American history, one must understand how God worked in Europe to bring about the colonization of the New World.

Since the dawn of Christianity, true believers have sought genuine freedom to worship God according to the dictates of the Bible. From the time of Christ, there have been three basic hindrances to Christianity. First was the access to Scripture. Until the entire canon of Scripture was determined, the believer only had access to a small part of the Scripture, possibly a gospel or an epistle. Once the Bible was complete, only the wealthy could access the Scriptures, due to the cost of transcription. In the Middle Ages, a scribe could work for six months laboring only on a single copy of Scripture. The other barrier to having the Scripture was that of language. For example, the English had no Bible in their language until the 1500s.

The second obstacle to freedom of religion has always been godless human government – first Rome, then the European nations that followed. From the time of Christ, His followers have cried out to governing powers as did the Israelites in bondage, "Let my people go," to worship God as their hearts and God's Word would dictate. The freedom cry swept across the European continent and finally washed up on the Atlantic coast of America with the founders of a new world in the seventeenth century.

Thirdly, suppression of religion has been an opponent to Christianity. The gospels and the book of Acts illustrate attempts to strangle Christianity in its infancy. But through persecution, the cause of Christ has thrived and spread to the uttermost parts of the Earth.

With these three obstacles in mind, a brief survey of Western history helps us to understand how and why God raised America to a place of prominence in world history. The marriage of a godless government and a harlot church by the year A. D. 400 led to continual persecution of Christians for the next millennium. By the mid 1200s, the Roman Church had established a court to try and punish religious dissenters. The Inquisition, as it was known, spread over southern Europe and terrorized believers for centuries. Anyone who sought freedom to worship and practice religion in a way different than the Catholic Church was subject to arrest and possibly death. Inquisitors were appointed from Rome with complete power to arrest anyone accused of heretical religious ideas. The Roman inquisitor acted as prosecutor, judge and jury. Often, trials were held in secret with the accused having no lawyer and no due process of law. It was not uncommon for an innocent person to confess to heresy to avoid the persecution of a trial and further punishment for claiming innocence. Inquisitors imprisoned hundreds of thousands, extracted false confessions, seized possessions and property from true believers, and sent thousands to their premature graves, all in the name of religion.

This was the world into which John Wycliffe was born. Wycliffe was an Oxford theology professor whose powerful preaching brought about a revival in England in the mid 1300s. He opposed the established church and preached that the essential doctrines of the Christian faith were the responsibility of the individual believer. He spent nearly two decades translating the Scriptures into English from the Latin Vulgate. Wycliffe openly challenged papal authority in England. Several times, the English reformer was summoned to defend himself in religious courts. He had amassed such a following that he was never convicted of heresy, and died of a stroke in 1384. Thirty-one years after his death, his remains were exhumed by order of the Council of Constance and burned. Wycliffe had started a fire in England that would spread to the whole of Europe, and eventually the New World.

The authority of Scripture that Wycliffe had preached would be propagated in Bohemia by John Huss. This doctrine alienated him from the Catholic Church. In 1415, he was called to the Council of Constance to defend his beliefs. The same religious court that ordered Wycliffe's remains burned condemned Huss to death for refuting the infallibility of the Pope, insisting on the authority of Scripture, and teaching the priesthood of the believer. While being burned at the stake, Huss cried out, "Lord, into thy hand I commend my spirit."[1] Once again, martyrdom fanned the flames of freedom in Europe.

As these fires of freedom sprang up across the continent, the message was the same – a call for reform and religious freedoms. But there was no way to carry the message to the masses. This all changed around 1440, when Johann Gutenberg developed a movable type printing pressing in Mainz, Germany. At once, the printed page carried ideas of freedom throughout Europe. Gutenberg realized the potential of his press. He stated the following:

> "Religious truth is captive in a small number of little manuscripts, which guard the common treasures instead of expanding them. Let us break the seal which binds these holy things; let us give wings to truth that it may fly with the Word, no longer prepared at vast expense, but multitudes everlastingly by a machine which never wearies-to every soul which enters life!"[2]

In 1456, Gutenberg produced the first edition of the Bible from the Latin Vulgate. In 1516, Desiderius Erasmus printed his first edition of the New Testament in Greek. By the time of his death, scholars had translated the Scriptures into several other languages, and the printing press was spreading the message of hope and freedom to pauper and prince throughout Europe.

The sparks and embers of religious freedom that dotted the continent at the beginning of the sixteenth century were about to become a full blaze in 1517 on the steps of a Catholic Church in the quiet college town of Wittenberg, Germany. A Catholic friar named John Tetzel, a personal representative of Pope Leo X, was crisscrossing Germany selling indulgences. These papal certificates excused a person from doing penance and shortened one's stay in Purgatory after death. The sale of these indulgences not only benefited the purchaser in the next life, but also helped finance the construction of the great St. Peters Cathedral in Rome. The lavish abuses of the Catholic Church claimed many, but the unscriptural sale of favors in this life and the next angered more. When Tetzel reached Wittenberg in October 1517, a young university professor named Martin Luther could remain silent no longer. Luther, a Catholic monk, had come to the knowledge of Jesus Christ as his personal savior, based on the Scripture proclaiming that "the just shall live by faith" in Romans 1:15. He boldly challenged Tetzel, the Pope, and the entire Catholic Church by nailing his 95 theses to the door of the church at Wittenberg. Though the practice of placing your religious beliefs on paper and on the door of the church was common, to challenge the church so blatantly was not. Leo X demanded that Luther appear before him in Rome and that he immediately retract his theses. The defiant monk refused both. Instead he wrote more. He published pamphlets and books and continued to teach salvation by grace and faith. In 1521, he was excommunicated from the Roman Catholic Church and outlawed by the Holy Roman Empire. His defense was plainly stated.

> "Unless I am convicted by Scripture and plain reason-I do not accept the authority of popes and councils, for they have contradicted each other-my conscience is captive to the Word of God. I cannot and I will not recant [take back] anything, for to go against conscience is neither right nor safe. God help me. Amen."[3]

The terror of the Inquisition had been broken and religious freedom was intoxicating the German people. Luther was a hero. He went on to publish more books and hymnals, to translate the Bible into his native tongue, and to establish churches. His protest became a movement. The Reformation had begun.

Ulrich Zwingli, a Catholic priest, fanned the flames of the reformation in Switzerland in the early 1500s by preaching the Bible as the sole rule of faith and practice for believers. Zwingli passed the mantle of Swiss religious leadership to John Calvin, who broke from the Catholic Church just after Zwingli's death. In 1536, he published his exhaustive work entitled *The Institutes of the Christian Religion*. Five years later, Calvin established a theocratic regime in Geneva, based on the Old Testament model of government. Though not perfect, Calvin's religious and governmental skills did pioneer a new type of religious freedom in Europe. Hundreds of reformers flocked to Switzerland to study under Calvin. It was from Geneva that John Knox carried the embers that would ignite the Scottish Reformation. Also from the Swiss Alps and the teaching of John Calvin came Menno Simons and the Anabaptist movement. These radicals called for only believers to be baptized, thus their name, which means "re-baptizers." The blaze of religious freedom was spreading across Europe, fanned by the zealous preaching of a few, the brave stand by many, and the printed Word of God.

While reformation swept across the continent, Protestantism gained a strong foothold in Rome's farthest outpost, England. This island fortress was the melting pot of Europe. Its language was diverse and profoundly non-romantic. Its government had evolved from feudalism to a system of written law based upon the Magna Carta of 1215, which insured the British certain basic but revolutionary freedoms, based upon the rule of law instead of the whim of the ruler. In fact, the king was bound by the law as well as the people. England's religion, however, though tainted with Celtic flavor, was still profoundly Roman. Wycliffe's followers, the Lollards, or poor preachers as they were called, carried on his work in the fourteenth century, but England did not embrace the reformation when Germany did in the 1520s.

In 1509, Henry VIII came to power in England at the age of 18. By this time, English law had eroded and Roman Catholicism was strongly entrenched in society. In 1520, Henry savagely attacked Luther's teachings and defended the authority of the papacy in his book entitled *Defense of the Seven Sacraments*. Pope Leo rewarded the English monarch by bestowing him the title "Defender of the Faith." Henry, staunchly Catholic and ruling with the divine right of kings, openly persecuted English religious dissenters. He had solicited and received permission of the Pope to marry his deceased brother's wife, Catherine of Aragon. The royal couple had six children but no male heir to the throne. By 1525, Henry sought to dissolve his marriage to Catherine, based upon the idea that God had disapproved of the union (Leviticus 20:21). He petitioned the Pope for an annulment.

> There were serious political ramifications in allowing Henry to divorce his first wife and marry another. Catherine of Aragon was the youngest daughter of Ferdinand of Aragon and Isabella of Castile-the Spanish monarchs who had sponsored Christopher Columbus' voyages of discovery to America. Catherine was also the aunt of the Holy Roman Emperor, Charles V. Furthermore, the Papacy had blessed Henry's and Catherine's marriage as being of God. Such a reversal would be embarrassing for the Vatican. The Pope sent Cardinal Lorenzo Campeggio as a Papal legate to research the matter of the king's marriage. Cardinal Campeggio conferred with Thomas Cromwell and Cardinal Wolsey, Archbishop of York and the head of the English church. The two Roman Catholic

clerics procrastinated until Henry was furious with impatience.[4]

Upon the suggestion of the reformer Thomas Cranmer, Henry appealed to the Catholic universities of Europe to rule on the Biblical authority to dissolve the marriage. This put the King of England in direct defiance to the Papacy in Rome. In 1532, English parliament granted Henry his divorce. He quickly married Anne Boleyn, which brought about a total separation with the Catholic Church. Henry was appointed the supreme head of the English Church and the English Catholic clergy were forced to submit to English rule. England had broken from Catholicism, but would struggle with this independence for several bloody decades. Though never fully extinguished, the fires of religious freedom that once burned low were suddenly brought to blaze by the selfish and sinful desires of a corrupted, tyrannical king. What a miracle! The defender of the "Catholic faith" founded his own faith, which became the spark that jumped the Atlantic and became a consuming fire that is still ablaze five centuries later.

5

The Protestant Wind

The Protestant Reformation was in full force by the last quarter of the sixteenth century. Nowhere was the reformation more pronounced than in England. Henry VIII had opened the great chasm between his Anglican Church and the Roman Catholic Church. His royal successor had further polarized the English people by insisting the country follow each sovereign's own religious practices. Edward, Henry's son, ruled in his father's stead as a Protestant. Upon his death, Mary, the first daughter of Henry, who was Catholic like her mother Catherine of Aragon, revived the practices of Catholicism as she ascended the throne in 1553. Bloody Mary, as she was known, martyred hundreds of Protestants, loyal to the Scriptures and opposed to the Pope in Rome. The following year, she married Philip II of Spain, further strengthening the ties to Catholicism. But in 1558, Mary died, leaving no heir. Her stepsister, Elizabeth, the daughter of Henry and Anne Boleyn, became queen and once again permanently changed the course of English history. She was strong-willed, dearly loved by her subjects, and extremely Protestant. England faced some of its gravest days, but was extremely blessed to have "Good Queen Bess," as she was affectionately known, at her helm.

As the English and Spanish were preparing to face off in a battle of Protestant and Catholic powers, the Dutch had been struggling with the Spanish for years. The Netherlands first came under the Hapsburg rule in 1477. Charles, the Hapsburg king of Spain, brought the Dutch under Spanish control in 1516. Fifty years later, Philip II came to power at the time that Protestantism was spreading across Europe. Ten years into his reign, 200 Dutch noblemen formed a league to oppose the Spanish Inquisition in Holland. When Philip refused to hear the cry of his Protestant Dutch subjects, 8,000 were executed and another 30,000 had their property confiscated. The Dutch declared themselves independent of Spain and Catholicism and founded the Dutch Reformed Church. Their sentiments were "The people were not created by God for the sake of the Prince...but, on the contrary, the Prince was made for the good of the people."[1] Fighting ensued, and the fear of annihilation loomed across the Dutch lowlands for a decade. Their only hope against the twin tyrants of Spain and Rome was Protestant Elizabeth of England. In 1586, she dispatched 6,000 troops in defense of Protestantism and to deny the Spanish a base from which to invade England. This move guaranteed war with Spain, but ironically ensured an English victory at the same time. Without a staging area for troops, the Spanish plans of invasion had to be drastically altered. They had to transport their entire invasion force from Spain by ship, defeat the English on sea, then land their army and fight the English on their beaches. This was a military plan that would never materialize.

By the 1580s, Spain was at the zenith of its power. Ships continuously unloaded valuable trade goods and precious metals, bestowed from her colonies in the New World. The shipments of gold and silver were of special interest to English privateers who roamed the Spanish Main, seeking to devour what the Spaniards had exploited from the Americas. With Elizabeth's blessings, captains such as Francis Drake and John Hawkins pillaged Spanish settlements and plundered Spanish shipping. Even though the Spanish were the first to raid English ships (in 1567, the Spanish attacked Hawkins's fleet), the British sea dogs quickly lapped up great successes against Spanish merchant ships. In 1580, Drake became the first captain to successfully circumnavigate the globe. (Magellan died while attempting the same feat in 1521.) Upon his return to England, Pirate Drake looted and captured the Spanish seaport of Cadiz, along with 30 ships. The mighty Spanish Empire was almost at the mercy of these English privateers. The answer was first proposed to Philip II in 1585 by the Marquis of Santa Cruz. His proposal was to amass a mighty flotilla, sail to England, and place a mighty landing force on English shores to bring the English to their knees before the sovereign Spanish king. Once the invasion plan was approved, years of planning and preparation were invested in the prospect of success. English coastal maps and routes of inland invasion had to be developed. Espionage agents in the British Isles were employed to develop a strategy to conquer the heathen dissenters of England. English Catholics were contracted to produce a base of loyalists on the fortress island. But it was essential that the invasion be kept a secret. It is almost ironic that the English learned of the proposed invasion from its embassies in Rome. Philip sought the blessings of the Pope in this military action, and it was a leak in the Vatican that sounded the alarm to the Protestant Queen Elizabeth. Espionage, political intrigue, and military coup were all the order of the day. In 1586, there were fears of a plot to assassinate Elizabeth and give the throne to her cousin, Mary. The Catholic Mary, Queen of Scots, would have undoubtedly appealed to the Spanish Philip to unite the two kingdoms under Romanism. This plot failed when Mary was executed on February 8, 1587. Philip remarked in a letter which may have been meant for the Pope:

> 'I am grieved,' he wrote, 'since...[Mary] would have been the most suitable instrument for leading...[England] back to the Catholic faith. But since God in His wisdom had ordained otherwise, He will raise up other instruments for the triumph of His cause.'[2]

Without a doubt, subtle espionage had failed. The Spanish would call for an all-out assault on their wayward brothers of English descent.

The invincible Armada was to be composed of four types of ships. First, the Spanish Navy would refit older ships and prepare them for war. Secondly, the navy called for a hasty construction of warships to be placed into immediate service. Since the invasion called for placing large numbers of soldiers, not sailors, on English soil, barges would be employed to ferry soldiers from the beaches of Calais across the English Channel to the English front. Lastly, Philip would rent ships from other countries to help invade the British Isles. In all, by the summer of 1588, the Armada amassed 130 ships and nearly 30,000 men of war, mainly soldiers, commanded by the Duke of Medina Sidonia.

With the element of surprise gone, and unable to place a force on Dutch soil just across the North Sea from England, Spanish hopes rested alone in their invincible Armada. Medina Sidonia would sail into the English Channel and take on the inferior British navy, secure a proper port, and land his troops on English soil. Though he was not as convinced as King Philip, both believed this was God's direct plan. They must deliver the wayward English from their sins against Romanism.

"At the highest levels of command, the Spanish expedition was seen as something very close to a crusade – that is a war hallowed by remission at least of the temporal consequences of the participants' sins."[3] The Spanish commander sought formal papal indulgences for his crusading Armada. He exhorted his men, "The saints of heaven will go in company with us, and especially the holy patrons of Spain, and, indeed those of England who are persecuted by the heretics and cry aloud to God for vengeance."[4] The belief that the invading army was on a mission for God was taught to the soldier as well. "The men of the fleet were exhorted to save the tender child who suckled on the poison of heresy, and doomed to perdition unless deliverance reaches them betimes."[5]

The idea of a grand crusade to free the rebellious English of the heresy against Rome must have actually originated with Phillip himself. Felipe Fernandez-Armesto states the following:

> Unless one discounts, on grounds of calculation and insincerity, everything he ever said on the subject, one must accept that Philip II saw history as providentially regulated and the Armada as part of God's work. During the approach to the campaign, he spent two or three hours every day 'on his knees, before the sacrament.' Juan de Vitoria was in no doubt that the higher figure was correct. The king ordered 'continual' prayers at court and urged them in the fleet. When the expedition was over and the scale of the disaster known, he wrote to the bishops of his realm, counting himself 'well served' by a programme of prayer, which, if it had not brought victory, must be presumed to have limited the scope of the catastrophe, and ordering a final solemn mass of thanksgiving in every church.

In his first instructions to Medina Sidonia he stressed, as the first priority, the need to preserve the participants in the expedition in a state of grace, communicated, confessed, and alert against sin, as in the old crusading tradition, in pursuit of divine favour and hence of victory: 'because victories are gifts of God... since you bear a cause which so much His own that He therefore makes promise of His favour and help, if not foregone by sinfulness, you must take great care that, in the Armada, sins are avoided.[6]

The Armada must be invincible since God himself had ordained its mission. Amazing as it may seem, Philip was seeking to emancipate the same people in England that he was persecuting in Spain-Protestants.

By the end of May, 1588, the Spanish fleet set sail from Lisbon harbor. The crusade for Spanish conquest of England began at the chief seaport of Portugal, and for many ended on the seashore of Iceland. The Armada forfeited an opportunity to trap the English fleet at Plymouth on July 19, but Medina Sidonia followed his orders to sail up the English Channel. At this point, Dutch gun boats blockaded the harbor at Dunkirk, preventing any Spanish soldiers from joining the Armada. The two fleets engaged in impromptu sparring matches for days in the channel. Several ships would fire at each other, then withdraw, usually without any significant results. The British appeared to be content to be on the defensive and to pour shot into the Spanish while the Armada waited for the proper time to do God's bidding. For example, there was no action at all on August 5 or 6, and only a little on other days. In the early morning hours of August 8, the English loaded eight wooden ships with explosives and set them ablaze, and a skeleton crew steered them toward the anchored Armada. The plan was to strike several ships and the explosions would damage or sink others. The end result was minimal. Several Spanish ships cut their anchors and frantically sailed away, but none were lost. The Spanish fleet was separated however; thus it was no longer intact. The British moved in for the kill. The attack was led by the old sea dog, Sir Francis Drake. Admiral Lord Howard had divided his fleet into three commands – one under Drake, another under Drake's cousin, John Hawkins, and the third led by Martin Frobisher. Drake's initial attack proved futile, but as the day wore on, the British fleet inflicted significant damage to the Spanish Armada. Two Spanish ships were lost, and several more limped away in a slow retreat to safety in the North Sea. This great sea battle that changed the course of history still remains an enigma. Why did the Spanish not do what they sailed to England to do – fight to liberate the Catholics of the British Isles while defeating the heathens of Protestantism? Why did the British not press the attack and force the Spanish to fight? It appears that invaders sailed off without any attempt to invade England at any point. The whole island could not have been defended. Fernandez-Armesto makes his point in this way.

The result, however, was far from satisfactory from an English point of view. By the most significant standard-that of objectives fulfilled or disappointed-the battle of 8 August, so often acclaimed as an English triumph and even as one of the decisive episodes in the history of sea power, was a Spanish victory and an English defeat. The Spaniards had achieved their purpose: the Armada was saved. The English had failed in theirs: it escaped, scotched but not killed. Howard thought that he had only 'plucked its feathers'. The Spaniards, though apprehensive about how long their fleet could remain battle-worthy, were willing to renew the fight next day.[7]

The battle appears to be inconclusive. What happened prior to and following the battle appears to be of great importance. There was a "storm," or in fact several storms that surrounded the events of 1588. In June, as the Armada was sailing toward England, it experienced a storm that prompted King Philip to reassess his crusade to England.

If this war were unjust, the storm might be understood as a sign that Our Lord's will were to desist from offending Him; but since it is so just as it is, we must not believe that He would withhold His protection from it, but rather favour it beyond our desires. But if it should prove to be His will to reserve for Himself the punishment of those people, then, accordingly, His Majesty's intention will have been fulfilled on his part by having striven to serve God with all the power which He has granted him in defense of His cause.

The enemies of the Catholic religion would interpret the damage inflicted by the storm as authority for their heresies, twisting in their favour God's tolerance, which was perhaps intended to chastise our sinfulness, or perhaps to enhance His glory at the time of our future successes. No step must therefore be taken by us to interrupt the course of the Divine purpose.[8]

The crusade continued. Following the fight of August 8, the English hoped to force the Spanish onto the shoals at Flanders, but the wind shifted, granting the Armada the ability to steer into the North Sea. This "Catholic Wind" allowed the Armada to regroup, remain intact and sail away to safety. Or did they?

Once in the Atlantic the Armada faced its toughest battle to date, another unseasonable storm. Many of the ships were already damaged due to the battle. Several could not keep up and others were lost at sea. The flotilla quickly became detached. Many ships must have perished on the rocky shores of Scotland and Iceland. Others miraculously managed to limp back to Spanish ports. In all, 63 of the 130 ships of the invincible Armada were lost. Their remains were strewn from the English Channel to the rocky slopes of western Iceland to the depths of the north Atlantic. The Protestant bastion of hope was saved. Queen Elizabeth stated, "He made the winds and waters rise to scatter all mine enemies."[9] Phillip's response is said to have been that he sent his Armada "against men, not against the sea and the weather."[10]

To the Spanish, God "allowed" the wind. To the English, God directed the wind. John Hawkins's presupposition of the attack was true.

> 'In open and lawful waters,' wrote Hawkins to Walsingham in February 1587, 'God will help us, for we defend the chief cause, our religion. God's own cause; for if we would leave our profession and turn to serve Baal (as God forbid, and rather to die a thousand deaths), we might have peace, but not with God.'[11]

6

The Forbidden Book

At the same time the Spanish and the Portuguese were expanding and exploiting their holdings in the heathen Americas, they were persecuting Christians, Jews, and other non-Catholics in their own homelands. In the first half of the sixteenth century, Europe became increasingly more Catholic. But the tide was to turn in 1517, when Martin Luther boldly nailed his 95 theses to the chapel door in Wittenburg, Germany, proclaiming "the just shall live by faith." This opened the floodgates of the Protestant Reformation that would spread over all of Europe, and eventually reach the shores of America by the end of the century.

This was just a beginning, if a beginning can ever be truly determined. Each historical event is always laid upon the foundation of a previous event, thought, or deed. The English reformation needed a catalyst to propel it to the forefront of English life – a rallying point from which to rally the troops for a holy war, an energy source more powerful than mortal man.

Wycliffe, the "Morning Star of the Reformation," had long since died. His "poor preachers," called Lollards or "idle babblers,", carried the light as far as human energy could go, but through decades of constant persecution, their message had fallen on deaf ears. They had become nearly invisible in Britain by the 1500s. The wicked, adulterous Henry, though king of England, was not the leader of God's church. Archbishop Cranmer would only serve to do Henry's prompting. England needed direction, spiritual direction, and she found it in a book.

William Tyndale was born in Gloustershire, England, just two years after Columbus's great discovery. He was educated at Oxford and Cambridge under the tutelage of Erasmus, who published his Greek New Testament during that time. While at Cambridge, Tyndale joined the White Horse Bible study.

> The membership names in that Bible study reads like a 'Who's Who" of the Reformation. It included the names of Clark, Frith, Barnes, Ridley, and Latimer. It produced two archbishops, seven bishops, and eight martyrs. Their common experiences, and unanimous conclusions, deeply impressed William Tyndale. The members of the White Horse fellowship considered access to the Word of God, and its unquestioned authority, as mandatory for any emancipation from religious shackles.[1]

The young Tyndale noted that the English people were not moved by their meaningless church services and liturgical repetitions. The masses did not comprehend the mass in Greek or Latin. His desire became the translation of the Bible into the common English language. "If God preserves my life, I will cause a boy that driveth a plow to know more of the Scriptures than the Pope."[2] But there were obstacles. First, law demanded that religion be communicated in Latin. In 1519, a group of English Christians had been burned at the stake for teaching children the Lord's Prayer and the Ten Commandments in their native tongue. Secondly, the law prohibited anyone from translating Scripture without the approval of the bishop. He was promptly refused this license by Bishop Cuthbert Turnstall. Not to be denied, Tyndale sought refuge on the continent at Wittenberg, Germany, the home of Martin Luther. He enrolled at the university using an alias, and worked on his translation of the New Testament into English.

> In the latter days of 1525, a few thousand copies of the complete New Testament were printed. The forbidden books were smuggled into England by merchant adventurers in the late winter and spring of 1525-26. Concealed in bags of flour and bales of cloth, they were received at the port of London which was, miraculously, under control of Germans.[3]

Immediately King Henry VIII condemned the translation and ordered it burned. The king and the church were so incensed by Tyndale's work that they paid four times the cost of the work to purchase it for burning. At that rate, Henry was paying Tyndale to print his New Testament and three out of four were reaching the hands of spiritually hungry Britons. Tyndale lived another decade as a fugitive on the mainland of Europe. He was arrested and condemned to death as a heretic in 1536. On the day of his execution, he proclaimed, "I call God to record that I have never altered, against the voice of my conscience, one syllable of His word. Nor would I this day, if all the pleasures, honors, and riches of the earth might be given to me." As he was being fastened to the stake, he cried out with these final words, "Lord, open the King of England's eyes."[4] Tyndale's uncompleted Old Testament translation was completed by two of his associates, Myles Coverdale and John Rogers. The latter was given permission to publish the Tyndale Bible under the pen name of Matthews, the year after the martyr's death. In 1539, Coverdale was granted permission by Henry to publish and distribute the "Great Bible" to every church in England. God did answer Tyndale's dying prayer to open the king's eyes. The wicked Henry required that an English Bible be chained to the pulpit of churches in his domain. Tyndale's life was over, but his work continues to this day. "So scholarly was Tyndale's work that it has been estimated that our present English Bible retains 80 percent of his original work in the Old Testament, and 90 percent in the New."[5]

The Tyndale translation caused an awakening in England, but Henry's repackaged Catholic Church held the people in liturgical bondage. God used the capricious Henry VIII to wrestle the church from the hands of the Pope, but in 1547, that control would pass to his nine-year-old son, Edward VI. The young monarch's uncle, Edward Seymour, became lord protector and sole guardian of the king. Under his control, and in part due to the Puritans who sought to purify the Church of England, Protestantism was firmly entrenched in the land.

Edward died in 1553, leaving the throne to his sister Mary, the daughter of Henry and Catherine of Aragon. The new Queen detested the church reforms made under Edward, as well as the break with the Roman Church under her father, and appealed to the Pope for a reconciliation. She appointed Catholic bishops and confined dissenters to the Tower. Against the wishes of Parliament, and after suppressing a brief Protestant rebellion, Mary wed the future King Philip II of Spain. "The marriage restored the Catholic creed, revived the laws against heresy, and attempted to enforce the wholesale conversion of the realm."[6] Pope Julius III appointed Reginald Pole as his legate in England. Before Parliament, he formally reunited the English and Roman churches and absolved the Lords and Commons of their sins. In secret, he established a prohibition on the printing of "vernacular" or non-Latin Bibles and the reading of Scripture in church. Mary's reign of terror had begun. By the time of her death in 1558, nearly 400 dissenters had been killed, 288 at the stake, of which John Rogers was the first. For five years, cries of the martyrs ascended to heaven as "Bloody Mary" enslaved the English in the bondage of Catholicism.

Her stepsister, Elizabeth reigned following Mary's death. So diametrically different was she that her subjects affectionately referred to her as "Good Queen Bess." Because of her religious toleration, many of the Pilgrims and Puritans who fled England during Mary's persecution returned from the mainland. Those who returned from Switzerland brought with them a relatively compact and affordable English translation of the Scriptures. "The Geneva Bible would become the Bible of the masses. Since it was also the first English Bible to be divided into chapter and verse, it proved to be a good study Bible."[7] Elizabeth's tolerance had so distanced the English Church from Rome that Pope Pius V formally excommunicated her as the "Pretended Queen of England, the serpent of wickedness, and declared her deposed, absolving her subjects from their allegiance to her."[8] The Pope even encouraged the assassination of "Good Queen Bess." This did not happen, and Elizabeth died an elderly queen in 1603, a decade and a half after she witnessed the Spanish Armada defeated, the last Catholic threat to her throne turned away.

Elizabeth's "cousin of Scotland," James, became King of England in 1603. He had been raised as a Presbyterian and gave the Puritans his ear in religious matters. By the turn of the seventeenth century, British Protestantism had several factions. The Anglican Church encompassed old line Catholics, the Puritans who sought to purify the church, and the Pilgrims who demanded separation from the main ecclesiastical body. James sought to appease all factions and at his suggestion, a new uniform translation of the Bible was authorized. This version would be the first English Bible to be translated by a committee. Six panels of translators, 47 in all, were entrusted with the task. Three panels worked on the Old Testament, two on the New Testament and one on the Apocrypha. Completed in 1611, the King James or Authorized Bible quickly became the Bible of the English.

It was the Scriptures that empowered the English to rise and unite for their freedoms. It was William Tyndale who brought the Scriptures to England. His prose and creativity in designing our language is the most grossly overlooked contribution to western civilization in the annals of our history.

> In his translation of the Bible, Tyndale wittingly shaped the English language so that a mental picture would form in the mind of the reader as he read the message of the text. At that time, the masses were the victims of tyranny from the religious establishment and the state. That tyranny denied them the freedom to own, read or memorize God's Word in the vernacular and, worse, necessitated an earthly advocate for God's children to relate to their Creator. As in the first century, 1,500 years earlier, the Church of Jesus Christ operated underground. Freedom in Christ existed in spite of the Inquisition.

Tyndale sought every possible expression to illuminate the message. It was the spiritual nature of man that he attempted to awaken in the reader. The apostle Paul had directed his message to the innermost man, the one that was distinguished from the physical body and soul. To know God and to experience God was in the spiritual dimension. The contest for man was not a warfare of flesh and blood, but of principalities and powers. Tyndale lived and translated like a first century believer, knowing that if he was captured, martyrdom was assured. Tyndale's word order and cadence touched the reader's spirit, then and now, and allowed him to know and trust in Whom he believed.[9]

7

God Has a Plan

Five years after Columbus's maiden voyage to the New World, John Cabot, an Italian sailing under the British flag, landed in North America. He was the first documented European to set foot on the North American mainland. Although Cabot was unsuccessful in his mission to find a water passage to the Orient, he did provide England a claim in the New World. However, the vast North American continent lay basically unclaimed for nearly a century. During that eventful century, England was reborn in her own reformation of religious thought.

As the sixteenth century dawned, America seemed destined to be Spanish-speaking and Roman Catholic. Just as God sent a wind to blow the Spanish Armada off course and on to ruin, God also planted the seeds of America's hope for liberty and freedom in England, thereby abandoning Spain in His search for a people to carry the Gospel to the regions beyond. In the 1500s, England seemed to be an unlikely place for religious freedom to be born. The monarchy vacillated from strong Anglican to Catholic sentiments. Their common bond was intolerance for any other dissenters or protestors of either church.

The rise of the middle class favored the growth of Protestantism. With fewer ties to tradition, merchants and artisans were ready conveyors of new ideas. It was due to the strength of this dynamic part of society in England that the Protestant countries such as Italy, where the middle class was similarly strong, can be understood by examining the Reformation's beginnings and growth in the sixteenth century England. When Luther's doctrine reached England about 1520, three years after the posting of his Wittenberg theses, it found a soil well prepared by 140 years of Lollard preaching. Lollardism, though bitterly suppressed, had never been uprooted. In fact, in the decade preceding 1520, it had become once again a serious threat to English Catholicism. Lutheranism, more than Lollardism, attracted the educated. It caught on at the universities, particularly at Cambridge, from which most of the English Protestant leaders were to come.

One of them, William Tyndale, conceived a plan to translate the Bible into English. When the church hierarchy proved hostile toward his project, Tyndale fled to the Continent, where in 1526 he published the first English

New Testament translated from the original Greek. (Wycliffe's version had been translated from the Latin Vulgate of Jerome.) In 1535 Tyndale was betrayed into the hands of the Spanish near Brussels, tried for heresy, and executed by strangling and burning.[1]

The blood of martyrs like Tyndale, Foxe and Bunyan cried out for religious tolerance. With little end in sight, God brought about another avenue of religious freedom, the colonization of America. The first English attempts at establishing settlements in the New World failed miserably.

The first expedition was led by Sir Humphrey Gilbert in 1578. Little is known of his exploits, but he did return to the Americas five years later, landing in Newfoundland briefly before sailing back to England. On the return trip, his ship sank during a storm near the Azores Islands. His half-brother, Sir Walter Raleigh, continued the daring explorations of British holdings in the New World. In 1584, Raleigh's ships reached the outer banks of what is now known as North Carolina. Arthur Barlowe and Philip Amadas led a landing party at Roanoke Island. They noted with amazement their welcome by the local chief's wife.

> She cheerfully came running out to meet us and commanded her people to pull our boats ashore. When we arrived at her house, she sat us down by the fire, took off our clothes, and washed and dried them...She herself

dressed meat for us, and we were entertained with all love and kindness and found the people most gentle, loving, faithful, and free of guile and treason, living in the manner of the golden age.[2]

Upon hearing the glowing report from Barlowe and Amadas, Raleigh named the country Virginia in honor of Elizabeth I, the Virgin Queen. She promptly knighted Raleigh and added her blessing to the colonization of Virginia. One hundred twenty colonists, led by Sir Richard Grandville, anxiously seized the opportunity to be the first English to settle in the New World. But once again, their aim seems to be gold not God. The initial settlers retreated to the comforts of England when Sir Francis Drake appeared at Roanoke the year after they arrived.

The colony established by Sir Walter Raleigh on Roanoke Island in 1585 collapsed when the aristocratic pioneers returned home to England. The next group of Raleigh's settlers landed two years later, but vanished before provisions and reinforcements could come from the mother country, due to the brief war with Spain in 1588. At this time, it appeared that God had no plan for the English to colonize the Americas.

In 1606, however, King James I granted a royal charter to the Virginia Company, later called the London Company, to colonize Virginia. Financing a venture of this magnitude was difficult for individual investors. The band of nearly 150 men left for America in December of 1606. After a rough Atlantic crossing, they sailed into Chesapeake Bay in the spring of 1607. Upon landing, Captain John Smith erected a wooden cross on the shores at Cape Henry and thanked God for their providential deliverance to the unknown land. Jamestown, named to honor the English monarch, was the first lasting tribute to James I, the first in a Stewart line of kings. Four years later, he is honored again with the completion of an English translation of the Bible that was to bear his name and be God's Word to the New World. The first charter of Virginia emphasized the Christian character of the expedition's purpose.

> "We, greatly commending, and graciously accepting of, their desires for the furtherance of so noble a work, which may, by the providence of Almighty God, hereafter tend to the glory of His Divine Majesty, in propagating of the Christian religion to such people as yet live in darkness and miserable ignorance of the true knowledge and worship of God, and may in time bring the infidels and savages living in those parts to human civility and to a settled and quiet government, do, by these our letters patent, graciously accept of, and agree to, their humble and well-intended desires."[3]

God providentially preserved the infant colony by using a teenage Indian girl named Pocahontas to save John Smith. She begged her father, Chief Powhatan, not to kill Smith. The Jamestown settlement may not have survived without the able leadership of John Smith or the merciful interventions of

Pocahontas. On another occasion, she brought food for the starving Englishmen.

The Jamestown experiment was flawed from its inception. Many of the gentry class, who came to Virginia strictly for financial gain, expected to become wealthy overnight, with little or no effort. They were not only unprepared for work, many did not work and died of starvation. Smith was convinced that no settlement could be sustained that ignored the Biblical principle, "if any would not work, neither should he eat." He lamented of the poor quality of workmen at Jamestown. "A hundred good workmen were worth a thousand such gallants."[4] He also established good "Christian" relations with the native tribes, treating them with respect. Jamestown survivor William Simmonds thanked the Almighty and the Indians for provision, as they "brought such plenty of their fruits and provision that no man wanted."[5]

Time and again, the struggling Jamestown colony was saved when things looked the bleakest. In 1609, Captain Samuel Argall saved the hungry settlers from starvation as he sailed up the James River with his small ship of provisions. That same year, King James granted a new charter for the colony and recalled John Smith to England. Due to the lack of success and constant struggle for survival, the parent company of the Jamestown experiment published a book entitled *A True and Sincere Declaration* to cover up the true story of the colony. Brown in *The Genesis of the United States* continued this coverup.

"(Our) principal and main ends...were first to preach and baptize into Christian religion and by propagation of the Gospel, to recover out of the arms of the Devil, a number of poor and miserable souls, wrapt up unto death in almost invincible ignorance; to endeavor the fulfilling and accomplishment of the number of the elect which shall be gathered from out all corners of the earth; and to add our mite to the treasury of Heaven."[6]

John Smith replied to the Virginia Company's propaganda in 1612 by releasing his *Description of Virginia,* which stated the following:

"We did admire how it was possible such wise men could so torment themselves and us with strange absurdities...making Religion their color when their aim was nothing but present profit, as most plainly appeared by sending us so many refiners, goldsmiths, jewelers, lapidaries, stone cutters...."[7]

Since the settlement had been re-supplied and settlers came and returned to England with each ship that sailed up the James, we will never know exactly how many settlers came, lived and died at Jamestown. But without the able leadership of John Smith, the colony looked doomed. William Simmonds wrote the following:

"The savages no sooner realized that Smith was gone, than they all revolted and murdered any white man they met...Now we all cried for the loss of Captain Smith, even his greatest enemies cursed his loss, for we had no more corn or contributions from the savages, but only mortal wounds from clubs and arrows. Of the 500 people left behind after Smith's departure, six months later there remained only 60 men, women, and children, most miserable and poor creatures, who survived on roots, herbs, acorns, walnuts, berries and now and then a little fish. So great was our famine that a savage we slew and buried was dug up by some and eaten...this is the time we called the starving time, which was too vile to describe and scarce to be believed..."[8]

All the livestock and food supplies were depleted. The Indians would not aid them and the "Christian colonists" had turned to cannibalism. On May 23, 1610, Thomas Gates, the king's appointee as governor of the colony, arrived to re-supply the colonists. He had been stranded on a deserted island near Bermuda for months, repairing his damaged ship. The newly appointed governor assessed the Jamestown situation while pondering the mystery of the Roanoke experiment, and then loaded all of his colony to return for England. Without making an attempt to continue the colony, he set sail for home. The Jamestown colony was a failure. As they sailed down the James River, they met three ships in the Chesapeake Bay.

Assuming that Governor Gates had perished at sea, Lord de La Warr (Delaware) had been appointed governor of the colony. He turned the beleaguered settlers around and returned to Jamestown. His first action was to organize a worship service and issue a Biblical call for personal sacrifice for both the new and established inhabitants of the colony. Jamestown was once again miraculously saved.

The settlement's salvation took on a different note this time – a spiritual one. Due to poor health, de La Warr returned to England and ruled the colony through a deputy, Thomas Dale. Dale quickly fused the spiritual and physical into law at Jamestown.

> They provided, for example, that every man and woman in the colony be forced to attend divine service (Anglican) twice a day or be severely punished. For the first absence the culprit was to go without food; for the second, to be publicly whipped; and for the third, to be forced to work in the galleys for six months...No other offense was more criminal than any criticism of the Thirty-Nine Articles of the Church of England. Torture and death were the lot of any who persisted in open criticism...[9]

Not to minimize the work of Pastor Robert Hunt, who ably pastored his Jamestown flock, but the spiritual climate of the infant colony changed drastically with the emergence of Thomas Dale as deputy governor. Whether by force or by faith, the colonists began to focus on their responsibilities toward God.

> The marriage of John Rolfe and Pocahontas revealed the evangelical spirit of the colonists. Rolfe wrote of his desire to see Pocahontas become a Christian: 'I will never cease until I have accomplished and brought to perfection so holy a work, in which I will daily pray God to bless me, to mine, and her eternal happiness.'[10]

Thomas Dale also established the right of private ownership of property to replace the ineffective communal system. Jamestown nearly failed due to the violation of God's principles of investment, hard work and return.

> The system of sharing labor and property was failing. The lazy people presumed, Dale complained, 'that howsoever the harvest prospered, the general store must maintain them.' Dale made it possible for the colonists to purchase their own land by either working part-time for the colony or contributing grain to the common store house. He thus established a system of private ownership that encouraged incentive. In so doing, he initiated the Biblical principle of individual ownership and responsibility-including hard work-that had helped to make America a prosperous nation. 'But they shall sit every man under

his vine and under his fig tree; and none shall make them afraid: for the mouth of the Lord of hosts hath spoken it' (Micah 4:4). 'But let every man prove his own work, and then shall have rejoicing in himself alone, and not in another' (Galatians 6:6). Jamestown still struggled for a few years, but it survived and soon prospered.[11]

Once the English settlers got their eyes off the promise of a quick, easy return on their money and began to trust in the principles of God's Word, the Jamestown colony began to thrive. God's Word and hard work worked. "The Christian religion was the underlying basis and the pervading element of all the social and civil institutions of the Virginia colony."[12]

The principles of free enterprise led to the need to organize the colony. The first representative assembly in America was instituted in the Jamestown church a dozen years after the colony was established. By that time, the Virginians had ventured far out of Jamestown and were inhabiting much of the Tidewater area of the state. They would meet in regular assembly to carry out the first European attempts at self-government in North America. This would be the forerunner of the American Congress. To open the inaugural assembly, Reverend Bucke led the Burgesses in prayer, seeking God's guidance in their proceedings.

In the infancy of the Jamestown experience, America's first permanent English colony, its inhabitants, though far from their homeland, honored God in every endeavor that they undertook. They planted the cross at Cape Henry when they first set foot on the Virginia shore. They built a house of worship and required mandatory attendance at religious services. They instituted representative self-government which honored and trusted God for their very existence. Through much trial and error, the English succeeded in planting a permanent settlement in America, thereby revealing that God did have a plan for the New World.

8

In the Name of God – Amen

The Separatist movement began in England in the late sixteenth century as a reaction to the state church's suppressive nature toward religion. In the tiny hamlet of Scrooby, in 1606, a group of Christian dissenters developed the first church covenant ascribing to self-government, separate and apart from the Church of England. It is from these humble beginnings in northern England that the Pilgrims trace their roots. The same year that colonists set sail for Jamestown, the Scrooby Separatists petitioned the king for permission to sail, not west to the new continent, but east to the old. As was the case for most English dissenters, a license to settle abroad was refused.

Another attempt to seek official permission for the Separatists to flee England was also denied in the spring of 1608. Later that year, these religious zealots devised a plan to flee their homeland without permission. A Dutch seaman agreed to transport them to Holland. Approximately 125 were on board the Dutch ship when British authorities arrived at the harbor to deny the sect's departure. The captain abruptly set sail with most of his passengers still on shore. Thus, these renegade Separatists of the Church of England started their pilgrimage with church hierarchy right on their heels. Families were separated, so some members were on board and others captive in England. Many left without cargo, belongings or family.

The group that we now know as the Pilgrims fled England in hopes of finding a better place to serve and worship God. They spent about a year in Amsterdam, then relocated in Leyden. Their formal application was accepted on February 12, 1609. The Dutch Burgomasters declared, "They refused no honest persons free ingress to come and have their residence in this city, provided that such persons behave themselves and submit to the laws and ordinances. Their coming will be agreeable and welcome."[1] When the British King James protested the Pilgrims fleeing to Holland and demanded their return, Jan Van Hout, the secretary of the city of Leyden, responded to the Royal, but made no effort to expel the refugees or to aid the king in apprehending them. In fact, the Pilgrims were quickly accepted in their new homeland. Due to their honesty and work ethic, Dutch bankers loaned them money and the newcomers thrived in the Dutch economy. The Dutch viewed the Pilgrims as human capital. William Bradford says this of the early Leyden experience.

"Being thus settled (after many difficulties) they continued many years in a comfortable condition, enjoying much sweet and delightful society and spiritual comfort together in the ways of God, under the able ministry and prudent government of Mr. John Robinson and Mr. William Brewster who was an assistant unto him in the place of an Elder, unto which he was now called and chosen by the church. So as they grew in knowledge and other gifts and graces of the Spirit of God, and lived together in peace and love and holiness and many came unto them from divers parts of England, so as they grew a great congregation."[2]

As time passed and families were reunited, the wayfarers enjoyed their new religious freedoms in Holland. The congregation thrived under the leadership of Pastor John Robinson. It also survived the Armenian controversy that shook the nation in the early 1600s. Jacobus Armenius was a professor of theology at the University of Leyden when the Pilgrims arrived. His strict opposition to the five points of Calvinism touched off great debates in the Netherlands. Pastor Robinson never became embroiled in the controversy and remained occupied with preaching three times weekly and publishing gospel tracts. It could have been here at Leyden that the Pilgrim belief system was galvanized and then taken to the New World.

The Pilgrims grew in responsibility and adapted to each new situation. They enjoyed freedom of religion and of self-government. Though they soared above doctrinal debates and remained pure in their beliefs, there were problems in Leyden. Bradford expressed four areas of grave concern to the Pilgrims.

1. They viewed Holland as a place where only a few English Separatists would come. "For many, though they desired to enjoy the ordinances of God in their purity and the liberty of the gospel with them, yet (alas) they admitted of bondage with danger of conscience, rather than to endure these hardships. Yea, some preferred and chose the prisons of England rather than this liberty in Holland."[3]
2. They realized that Holland would be an impossible place to realize a true Separatist colony. "So as it was not only probably thought, but apparently seen, that within a few years more they would be in danger to scatter,...and were fearful either to be entrapped or surrounded by their enemies so as they should neither be able to fight nor fly. And therefore thought it better to dislodge betimes to some place of better advantage and less danger, if any such could be found."[4]
3. They realized that they were losing their children to Dutch culture. "Many of their children, by these occasions and the great

licentiousness of youth in that country, and the manifold temptations of the place, were drawn away by evil examples..."[5]
4. They had a desire to win the lost in remote parts of the globe. "Lastly (and which was not least), a great hope and inward zeal they had of laying some good foundation...for the propagating and advancing the gospel of the kingdom of Christ in those remote parts of the world;..."[6]

In essence, the Pilgrims realized that they were ineffective foreign missionaries in Holland. They had not even converted the wicked Dutch into "keeping the Sabbath holy" as the fourth commandment of the Decalogue instructed. The strong-willed Dutch had begun to turn the hearts of the young English from the morals and ethics of their parents. The cost of freedom in Holland was too much. The Pilgrims must seek the promises of a new country as described in Hebrews 11:13-16:

These all died in faith, not having received the promises, but having seen them afar off, and were persuaded of them, and embraced them, and confessed that they were strangers and pilgrims on the earth. For they that say such things declare plainly that they seek a country. And truly, if they had been mindful of that country from whence they came out, they might have had opportunity to have returned. But now they desire a better country, that is, an heavenly: wherefore God is not ashamed to be called their God: for he hath prepared for them a city.

The God of providence sent the Pilgrims to Holland for a reason. This low-lying country that had been claimed from the sea was the staging area for God's people to carry the gospel to the New World.

The Dutch have given many things to America: Easter eggs, Santa Claus, waffles, sauerkraut, sleighing, skating and a host of 'vans' and 'velts; who helped to build our nation. But perhaps their greatest contribution to America was the eleven years of freedom they gave the Pilgrims — crucial years that helped America's founding fathers work out their philosophy of freedom and prepare for self-government in the New World...The eleven years the Pilgrims spent in Holland saw them grow in responsibility, adaptability, and self-government. As Bradford Smith put it in his biography of William Bradford, 'The libertarian tradition at Plymouth, with its profound influence on American life, is not primarily English. It is Dutch. Simple justice demands that we acknowledge this...Thus, during their Leyden years, were the Pilgrims perfecting themselves for the undreamed of work of founding a new nation. In religion, they grew milder and more tolerant. In business and craftsmanship they learned a great deal from the thrifty, ambitious, and highly capable Hollanders. Too, the Dutch flair for efficient government and record-keeping, the spirit of republicanism and civic responsibility were to bear unsuspected fruit in a distant land.'[7]

But where would that distant land be? William Bradford, in his seventeenth century work concerning the Pilgrims, states that they first considered Guiana as their promised land, but altered their plans to inhabit northern Virginia. In 1617, the Leyden congregation contacted the Virginia Company in London, expressing their desire to settle in America. They sent Robert Cushman and John Carver as their ambassadors to negotiate a suitable contract. Cushman and Carver carried the Pilgrim statement of purpose composed in seven articles. A brief synopsis follows:

1. Acknowledgement of the XXXIX Articles of Religion
2. Wish to keep spiritual communion with the Church of England
3. Acknowledge obedience to the King of England unless he commands them against "God's Word"
4 & 5. A somewhat qualified admission of the legality of bishops
6. Admission that no body can have ecclesiastical jurisdiction except by the king's authority

7. Agreed "to give all superiors due honor"[8]

The seven articles of purpose, the accompanying documents and possibly persuasive counsel from Cushman and Carver appear to have settled any questions about these religious dissenters and civil deserters. The Virginia Company seemed to be willing to transport and outfit them in northern Virginia, providing the congregation could offset some of the cost of the venture.

A Copy of Letter from Sir Edwin Sandys, directed to Mr. John Robinson and Mr. William Brewster.

After my hearty salutations. The agents of your congregation, Robert Cushman and John Carver, have been in communication with divers select gentlemen of His Majesty's Council for Virginia; and by the writing of seven Articles subscribed with your names have given them that good degree of satisfaction, which hath carried them on with a resolution to set forward your desire in the best sort that may be, for your own and the public good. Divers particulars whereof we leave to their faithful report; having carried themselves here with that good discretion, as is both to their own and their credit from whence they came. And whereas being to treat for a multitude of people, they have requested further time to confer with them that are to be interested in this action, about the several particularities which in the prosecution thereof will fall out considerable, it hath been very willingly assented to. And so they do now return unto you. If therefore it may please God so to direct your desires as that on your parts there fall out no just impediments, I trust by the same direction it shall likewise appear that on our part all forwardness to set you forward shall be found in the best sort which with reason may be expected. And so I betake you with this design (which I hope verily is the work of God), to the gracious protection and blessing of the Highest.

London, November 12 *Your very loving friend,*
Anno: 1617 *Edwin Sandys[9]*

On December 15, the Leyden congregation replied under the hand of John Robinson and William Brewster. This letter, directed to Edwin Sandys, expressed the Pilgrim motivation for the venture.

1. We verily believe and trust the Lord is with us, whom and whose service we have given ourselves in many trials; and that He will graciously prosper our endeavours according to the simplicity of our hearts therein.
2. We are well weaned from the delicate milk of our mother country, and inured to the difficulties of a strange hard land, which

yet in a great part we have by patience overcome.
3. The people are, for the body of them, industrious and frugal, we think we may safely say, as any company of people in the world.
4. We are knit together as a body in a most strict and sacred bond and covenant of the Lord, of the violation whereof we make great conscience, and by virtue whereof we do hold ourselves straitly tied to all care of each other's good and of the whole, by every one and so mutually.
5. Lastly, it is not with us as with other men, whom small things can discourage, or small discontentments cause us to wish themselves at home again. We know our entertainment in England and in Holland. We shall much prejudice both our arts and means by removal; who, if we should be driven to return, we should not hope to recover our present helps and comforts, neither indeed look ever, for ourselves, to attain unto the like in any other place during our lives, which are now drawing towards their periods.[10]

It took almost two years for the Pilgrims and the Virginia Company to come to terms and finalize plans for the voyage. On July 1, 1620, terms much like those of the Jamestown settlement were published. Each person 16 years of age or older would have a share in the venture for ten pounds sterling (approximately $700 in today's value). If a person outfitted and equipped himself, he would have another share. Those who wanted to buy extra shares could do so. The joint partnership would continue for seven years (the standard time of indenture). At the end of the term, all land and profits would be divided according to shares. Personal property, houses and improvements would remain the property of the shareholder who developed the lot. The Pilgrims were given two days off per week to do as they wished. All other days, work was for the profit of the company. All persons were to have their meat, drink, apparel and provisions from the common stock and good of the company.[11]

The venture would be comprised of two groups. The Pilgrims were known as planters. Another non-religious group, organized by Thomas Weston, was referred to by the Virginia Company as the adventurers.

The *Speedwell,* a small fishing boat, was purchased by the Leyden group to take with them to establish a small fishing enterprise. The *Mayflower* was hired to transport the planters and the adventurers. About 50 Pilgrims boarded the *Speedwell* and made the trip from Leyden to Southampton, England to join the *Mayflower.* Pastor John Robinson stayed behind in Leyden to pastor the home church and organize other passages to the New World. He placed Elder William Brewster as a non-ordained spiritual leader of the American group. Just before departure, Weston attempted to renegotiate the contract with the Pilgrims. They refused to revise the contract and Weston refused to pay the final payment for the voyage. To settle the debt, the Leyden Christians surrendered over 3,000 pounds of butter before sailing. On August 5, 1620, the two ships set sail from Southampton bearing saint and sinner alike, searching for a new life in a new world. Shortly out to sea, the captain of the *Speedwell* found his tiny ship so un-seaworthy that both ships returned to port at Dartmouth, England, for repairs. Once repairs were made, the mariners set out again, only to find the same problem at sea. Both ships returned to England, this time at Plymouth. The *Mayflower*'s captain and quarter owner, Christopher Jones, deemed the *Speedwell* un-seaworthy and loaded what he thought necessary onto his ship and set sail for America on September 6, 1620.

The unforeseeable delays put the weary Pilgrims later into the season than expected. There would be no crops for food. They would have to be resourceful and live off the land and whatever they took with them. Packed into cramped quarters and suffering from seasickness, the Leyden Christians were bound for their promised land, and along the way they witnessed the hand of God. First, the delays that seemed so heartbreaking for the passengers (loss of the ship, cost for repairs, departing without the Speedwell's supplies and the loss of a month) could very well have been a blessing, when you consider when and where they landed.

Secondly, William Bradford, who made the crossing, tells of a "proud and very profane young man" who constantly cursed and mocked the ailing Pilgrims. He gladly proclaimed that he longed for the day to cast the dead Christians' bodies overboard and claim their possessions as his own. "But it pleased God, before they came half seas over, to smite this young man with a grievous disease of which he died in a desperate manner, and so was himself the first that was thrown overboard. Thus his curses light on his own head, and it was an astonishment to all his fellows for they noted it to be the just hand of God upon him."[12]

Thirdly, Bradford mentions "many fierce storms" that oftentimes made the seasoned mariners doubt the fate of the voyage. These storms blew the *Mayflower* far north of her debated destination. The only historical statement as to the Pilgrims' intended place of settlement is a statement from William Bradford which mentions "some place about Hudson's River."[13] By virtue of their patent from the Virginia Company, the Pilgrims could settle at or near the mouth of the Hudson, but this would be the most northern extremity of the land grant. The Hudson River region was also claimed by the Dutch, due to Henry Hudson's exploration of 1609. In any case, the Pilgrims were pushing their luck when God blew them even farther north, past the Dutch claim and on to Cape Cod. The hand of providence in this location can only be seen in the events of the settlement of the colony.

When the Pilgrims arrived at the safe harbor after 65 days on the open seas, they fell upon their knees and thanked God for their safe passage. Scouting parties were sent out and discovered Indian dwellings and stores of corn.

> "And here is to be noted a special providence of God, and a great mercy to this poor people, that here they got seed to plant them corn the next year, or else they might have starved, for they had none nor any likelihood to get any till the season had been past, as the sequel did manifest. Neither is it likely they had had this, if the first voyage had not been made, for the ground was now all covered with snow and hard frozen; but the Lord is never wanting unto His in their greatest needs; let His holy name have all the praise."[14]

William Bradford, according to his writing and the footnotes by Samuel Morison in *Of Plymouth Plantation*, appears to have been in most of the early Pilgrim landing parties that searched for days for a suitable site to establish the settlement. His writings are replete with the providences of God in providing for the newcomers in the treacherous New England wilderness. In mid-December, the sea-weary Pilgrims all set foot on the New World at a place they called Plymouth, named for the last city that they saw in the Old World.

Before the Pilgrims departed the *Mayflower*, they realized their need for civil government. Since their charter with the Virginia Company gave them the right to settle in northern Virginia (At that time Virginia included territory from present-day Virginia to New York), they viewed themselves as beyond their legal charter and subject to self-government. Since they viewed each individual as depraved, civil government was a necessity. The Mayflower Compact was drawn and signed by 41 men on November 11, 1620. The signing took place as the *Mayflower* set in Providence town harbor before the Pilgrims explored the region. The covenant read as follows:

> "In the Name of God, Amen. We, whose names are underwritten, the Loyal Subjects of our dread Sovereign Lord King James, by the Grace of God, of Great Britain, France, and Ireland, King, Defender of the Faith, etc. Having undertaken for the Glory of God, and Advancement of the Christian Faith, and the Honor of our King and Country, a Voyage to plant the first colony in the northern Parts of Virginia; Do by these Presents, solemnly and mutually in the Presence of God and one another, Covenant and combine ourselves together into a civil Body Politick, for our better Ordering and Preservation, and Furtherance of the Ends aforesaid; And by Virtue hereof do enact, constitute, and frame, such just and equal Laws, Ordinances, Acts, Constitutions, and Offices, from time to time, as shall be thought most meet and convenient for the general Good of the Colony; unto which we promise all due Submission and Obedience. In WITNESS whereof we have hereunto subscribed our names at Cape Cod

the eleventh of November, in the Reign of our Sovereign Lord King James of England, France, and Ireland, the eighteenth and of Scotland, the fifty-fourth. Anno Domini, 1620"[15]

By the terms of this, the so-called Mayflower Compact, the Pilgrims agreed to govern themselves until they could arrange for a charter of their own. They were never able to arrange for such a charter and the Compact remained in force until their colony at Plymouth was absorbed in that of the Massachusetts Bay in 1691.[16]

The Compact was a binding agreement whereby its signers (41 of the 103 who set foot at Plymouth) agreed to govern themselves based upon their stated purpose – to plant a colony to glorify God and advance the Christian faith and to honor king and country. Their procedure was to form a civil body or government. Their plan was to organize and preserve the colony through the avenue of the government based upon submission and obedience. But the question is, submission and obedience to what or whom? Some would say that the Pilgrims and adventurers were only submitting to each other. But what of the king, the country and the Creator cited in the document? Others will affirm that the Compact was an agreement between man and God. The Pilgrims had already formally issued their statement of purpose to the Virginia Company. Now they were formally yielding to God as they had stepped outside the realm of civil authority into heathen America, where only God could protect and direct them. Could the Compact be a metaphor whereby the signers are actually submitting to both man and God, physically and spiritually at the same time? The best explanation seems to be that the signers, both sinner and saint, are yielding themselves to all levels of authority to make their colony productive. They were acknowledging all levels of voluntary civil government for the local "civil body politic" to the King of England and beyond. In fact, the final authority would be the Creator himself. Since the motivation for their mission was divine, they sought divine providence and direction on every hand. From the origin of their pilgrimage to the entrance of their promised land, their mission was "In the name of God, Amen: - so be it!"

Once the site of the town was chosen, work quickly began on civilizing the frontier. Streets were laid out, a common house for meetings was constructed, smaller dwellings were started and a stockade-type palisade was begun. This was all done in the dead of winter, with part of the party still on board the *Mayflower*. In fact, Captain Jones was invaluable to the settlers for months after they arrived. He pledged that he would stay in the harbor, approximately one-and-one-half miles from Plymouth, for as long as possible. He remained there until the Pilgrims got a foothold in the area and spring had come. He also left at least four cannons and a small sailing vessel, so the settlers could maneuver the coastline of the region.

The darkest hour for the fledgling colony was in the darkness of their first winter in America. In December, six died, probably from scurvy, exhaustion or pneumonia. In January, eight more succumbed to the rough American frontier. Several more sick Pilgrims nearly perished when the newly constructed common house caught on fire. By the end of the rugged first winter, 47 of the 102 people who left the comforts of Europe in August were dead. Thirteen of the 18 wives were dead, including Governor Bradford's wife, who fell overboard on the *Mayflower*. At one point in the frigid little palisade at Plymouth, only five men cared for the rest of the sick and dying. But the settlement survived. With a mortality rate at 46 percent, the Pilgrims fared far better than the first settlements at Roanoke, which lost all their inhabitants, and Jamestown, which suffered close to a 90 percent mortality rate. The Pilgrims not only survived, but also gave God the glory for what he had done. Unlike Jamestown, their struggles brought them closer to each other and to their Provider.

The Pilgrims remained steadfast in their belief that God had directed them to America. In spite of the devastating winter, when Captain Jones weighed anchor in April, not one Pilgrim returned to England with the *Mayflower*. God had divinely protected them, so they all stayed in America.

The remarkable providence of God can be seen as he sustained the Pilgrims on the initial year of their pilgrimage. The first act of providence was in the place of their landing. The delay in leaving England and the series of storms that the Mayflower encountered on her voyage drastically altered her destination, but God had a hand in this, as the Pilgrims found out in March of 1621. As they were thawing out from their first New England winter, a young Indian named Samoset bravely marched into their tiny town. He welcomed the foreigners to his land and in English asked, "Have you got any beer?" The startled Pilgrims fed the stranger and anxiously learned his story. He had learned English from English-speaking fisherman and fur traders who worked in the New England area. Samoset went on to explain the secrets of the region to the newcomers. He told them that the area was once inhabited by the Patuxets, a fierce tribe that had been decimated by an epidemic about three years before. That is why the land was cleared, but abandoned. The Pilgrims rejoiced in the providential preparations for their arrival in America.

Secondly, God's directing of Samoset to the Pilgrims led the Pilgrims to Massasoit, the chief of the neighboring Wampanoags. Massasoit and nearly 60 braves were led to Plymouth by Samoset. After a hearty meal and an exchange of gifts, the Wampanoags and Pilgrims agreed on a peace treaty that lasted 55 years. The treaty illustrated respect for the Indian and a Biblical view of life and property. Governor Bradford recorded the basis of the agreement.

1. That neither he nor any of his should injure or do hurt to any of their people.
2. That if any of his did hurt to any of theirs, he should send the offender, that they might punish him.

3. That if anything were taken away from any of theirs, he should cause it to be restored; and they should do the like to his.
4. If any did unjustly war against him, they would aid him; if any did war against them, he should aid them.
5. He should send to his neighbors confederates to certify them of this, that they might not wrong them, but might be likewise comprised in the conditions of peace.
6. That when their men came to them, they should leave their bows and arrows behind them.[17]

What a miracle to live at peace with your fellow man, even though you had invaded his territory and could not speak his language. "Massasoit was a remarkable example of God's providential care for His Pilgrims. He was probably the only other chief on the northeast coast of America who would have welcomed the white man as a friend."[18]

A third act of providence was the discovery of Indian corn, harvested and preserved in earthen mounds.

> These expeditions on discovery had this one remarkable smile of Heaven upon them; that being made before the snow covered the ground, they met with some Indian Corn; for which 'twas their purpose honestly to pay the native on demand; and this Corn served then for seed in the Spring following, which

else they had not been seasonably furnished withal. So that it proved, in effect, their deliverance from the terrible famine.'[19]

The Pilgrims viewed this as a gift from God. In fact, they tried as best they could to make treaties, barter and trade and purchase from the natives of America.

The fourth miracle was the appearance of the Indian Squanto along with Chief Massasoit. Squanto spoke English even better than Samoset. He was also the only known survivor of the Patuxet tribe. His story began in 1605, when he and others were taken captive by the Englishman George Weymouth, who was exploring the region. The Indians were taken to England where they learned to speak the new language. In 1614, Captain John Smith of Virginia fame returned Squanto to his native land while mapping the Cape Cod region. Before he could reacclimate himself to Patuxet life, he and 19 other Indians were captured by Captain Thomas Hunt and sold into slavery on the sea coast of Spain. Before the unwilling Squanto was shipped off to North Africa, he was purchased by a Catholic friar and introduced to "Christianity." From there he apparently escaped to England, where he caught another ship, captained by Thomas Dermer, and sailed back to New England. Miraculously, at Monhegan, Maine, the ship picked up Samoset. The two Indians met for the first time, not knowing of God's use for them in providing for the Pilgrims. Squanto arrived back on his native soil only to find no one. His entire tribe had been decimated by a plague. In despair, he joined himself to the Wampanoags and Massasoit who led him back to his homeland and the Pilgrims. Squanto continued to live with the Pilgrims. He taught the settlers how to fish, plant corn, till the field, stalk deer, refine maple syrup, and to trap beaver. The trading of beaver pelts became the financial life saver for the settlement.

The fifth act of God on behalf of His saints at Plymouth was in their survival. Many of the Pilgrims suffered on board the *Mayflower*. Scurvy and other common diseases affected the crew and passengers alike. Captain Jones lost nearly one-half of his crew on this trip to America. The four months that the *Mayflower* remained in Cape Cod were long and hard, but at the same time, those Pilgrims on shore were suffering beyond belief. With the death rate over 50% in Plymouth and at one point only a mere five men to care for the entire settlement, one can easily point to the hand of God as being their deliverance.

The sixth act of providence is mentioned by J. Steven Wilkins in his work, *America, the First 350 Years*. Simply stated, God took 47 settlers. They simply did not have enough food for all. It is highly possible that the entire settlement would have perished if the 47 had not died. Cotton Mather states the same in his history of the colony.

> And there was this remarkable providence further in the circumstances of this mortality, that if a disease had not more easily fetch so many of this number away to Heaven, a famine would probably have destroyed

them all, before their expected supplies from England arrived.[20]

The hand of God was not only evident in Plymouth, but it was recognized by the Pilgrims and openly spoken of by the early historians of the colony. Their days of thanksgiving to God and sharing with their Indian neighbors were also a testimony of God's grace and the Pilgrims' faith in God.

The second winter at Plymouth was extremely hard, for 35 more colonists landed in November with no extra food or provisions. Governor Bradford realized the gravity of the situation and began rationing the food. At one point, a daily food ration was reduced to five kernels of corn per person, but not one person died of starvation.

When spring came, the governor ordered that there be a second planting of corn – the first for the common store, the second for private use. Bradford realized the communal plan had no incentive to work. Since a Pilgrim had a depraved nature, he needed motivation to toil in the hot New England sun.

> ...it made all hands very industrious, so as much more corn was planted than otherwise would have been by any means the Governor or any other could use, and saved him a great deal of trouble and gave far better content. The women now went willingly into the field and took their little ones with them to set corn, which before would allege weakness and inability, whom to have compelled

would have been thought great tyranny and oppression.[21]

The spring of 1623 saw a great 12-week drought. The natives had not seen such and the Pilgrims became afraid for their own survival. A time of prayer and personal repentance was called over the entire settlement. Many must have thought of God bringing the Israelites out of bondage and then allowing them to die in the wilderness because of their own sin. God heard the Pilgrims' prayers and saw their repentance and granted his rain to water their fields. The spiritually observant governor notes more than a gentle summer rain.

> "It came, without either wind or thunder, or any violence, and by degrees in that abundance as that the earth was thoroughly wet and soaked therewith. Which did so apparently revive and quicken the decayed corn and other fruits, as was wonderful to see and made the Indians astonished to behold."[22]

The fall harvest was so great that year, that the thankful Pilgrims traded with their neighbors and proclaimed a second Thanksgiving feast. At this feast, a plate with only five kernels of corn sat before every joyous settler. Governor Bradford wanted all to remember how close things had been, and how God had blessed them.

9

A City Upon a Hill

By the dawning of the seventeenth century, the Protestant Reformation was a century old. The printing press was churning out page after page of religious materials and many European countries could read the Scriptures in their native tongues. Though Martin Luther had beaten the church doors open with his 95 theses, church hierarchy had succeeded in closing Heaven to many of its communicants. A century after Luther, and two-and-one-half centuries after Wycliffe, the English church still stirred little or no interest to the majority of Britons. They saw no need for a cold, lifeless expression of religion.

Then God began to move in the English church as He did in the time of Wycliffe and the Lollards. One by one, men began to rise up and call for a pure church. The religious dissenters became known by their motives – Puritans. They differed from the Pilgrims and Baptists who were strongly separatists in their views of the Church of England. The Puritans condemned those who would separate from the Church and sought to purify the institution from within. The problem was that they never possessed enough power to enact their reforms. While James I was on the throne, they were tolerated. In fact, in the translation of the Authorized Version of the Bible, the Puritans took an active part, but when James died in 1625, the Puritans were immediately ostracized. Charles I replaced James and appointed William Laud as the Archbishop of Canterbury. As the ruling bishop of the Anglican Church, he relegated the Puritan ministers to lesser roles in the church, then later, persecuted them outright. During this time of persecution, the Puritan movement was gaining momentum. The life-changing experience of salvation by God's grace, through the avenue of personal faith, energized new believers to share their faith with others, who in turn accepted Christ and continued the chain of sharing their faith. This revival of true Christian faith, linked with the access to the Scriptures in the English language, took away the dependence upon the church. It placed it squarely upon the believer. The believer had a need for Christian fellowship and service in a local church, but he was no longer bound to the church for salvation. The dissenters had a dilemma. Would they continue to attempt to revive a lifeless church, or separate from it to form a new, vibrant one? The struggle lasted for well over a quarter of a century. The Puritans honestly believed that they could reform the English Church and impact their society. They detested the Pilgrims who sailed away and left the problem church behind. Then the concerned Puritans developed a noble idea.

They could remain in the Church of England, but relocate to the New World. In principle, they were in the church, but in practice they were out – at least out of the reach of Bishop Laud, but still well within the grasp of God.

In 1628, the Massachusetts Bay Company was chartered and given a patent to establish a colony in America. John Endecott was sent with about 60 men to settle north of the Pilgrims in Massachusetts. Their first American winter was cold and dark, much like the Pilgrims' first. Endecott appealed to his Plymouth brethren for aid when it looked bleak for his fledgling colony. Governor Bradford sent a doctor, Samuel Fuller, who attended the sick and comforted the dying through the entire winter. The next year, several hundred more Puritans flocked to the new colony. In spite of the high mortality and desertion rate (several returned to England), Endecott insisted on calling his infant town Salem, which is Hebrew for peace. The Puritans would rather live in the ragged edge of civilization than to endure religious persecution in the civility of their homeland. They established their first church on August 6, 1629, by entering into a solemn covenant with God and one another.

> We covenant with our Lord, and one with another; and we do bind ourselves in the presence of God, to walk together in all his ways, according as he is pleased to reveal himself unto us in his blessed word of truth; and do explicitly, in the name and fear of God, profess

and protest to walk as followeth, through the power and grace of our Lord Jesus Christ.

We avouch the Lord to be our God, and ourselves to be his people, in the truth and simplicity of our spirits.

We give ourselves to the Lord Jesus Christ, and the word of his grace for the teaching, ruling and sanctifying of us in matters of worship and conversation, resolving to cleave unto him alone for life and glory, and to reject all contrary ways, canons, and constitutions of men in his worship..

Promising also unto our best ability to teach our children and servants the knowledge of God, and of His Will, that they may serve Him also; and all this not by any strength of our own, but by the Lord Christ: whose blood we desire may sprinkle this our Covenant made in his name.[1]

In 1629, the New England Company was reorganized as the Massachusetts Bay Company, and applied for a new charter. The expanded charter was approved by Parliament and signed by King Charles. The royal charter was unique in that every other charter called for the company to meet and be administered in England. The new Bay Company's charter did not specify the location of administration.

The Bay Company's partners were privately jubilant. There was now nothing binding them to England, nothing to prevent them from moving to New England themselves — and taking their charter with them. Once removed from the suspicious eyes of Church and Crown, the Company could become a self-governing commonwealth with the charter as its *carte blanche*. Only now, they would be governed by the laws of God, not merely the laws of men. Not since God had brought the first Chosen People into the first Promised Land had a nation enjoyed such an opportunity.[2]

A week after issuing the Massachusetts Bay Company charter, Charles seized absolute power in England and dissolved Parliament. God's hand of providence was on the Puritans. The exodus had begun, but who would He call to lead the new Israel?

The owners of the Bay Company had already found their man. His name was John Winthrop, an English squire. He was mature (about 40), successful, wealthy and a devout Puritan. But would he exchange a life of ease in England for one of suffering in America? Yes, indeed he would, just like the real Moses (Hebrews 11:25-26). Winthrop boldly stated his reasons for throwing his lot with the American dreamers and for sailing to the New World.

> It will be a service to the Church of great consequence to carry the Gospel into those

parts of the world, to help on the coming of the fullness of the Gentiles, and to raise a bulwark against the kingdom of Anti-Christ which the Jesuits labor to rear up in those parts.

All other Churches in Europe are brought to desolation, ... and who knows but that God hath provided this place to be a refuge for many whom he means to save out of the general calamity, and seeing the Church hath no place left to flee into but the wilderness, what better work can there be, than to go and provide tabernacles and food for her against she comes thither.

The Fountains of Learning and Religion are so corrupted as ... most children ... are perverted, corrupted, and utterly overthrown by the multitude of evil examples and the licentious government of those Seminaries, where men strain at gnats and swallow camels ...

It appears to be a work of God for the good of his Church in that he hath disposed the hearts of so many of his wise and faithful servants both ministers, and others not only to approve of the enterprise but to interest themselves in it ...[3]

In March 1630, Governor John Winthrop and his newly organized company set sail from Southampton with 11 ships bound for America. Reverend John

Cotton preached the farewell sermon that day from II Samuel 7:10 – "Moreover I will appoint a place for my people Israel, and will plant them, that they may dwell in a place of their own, and move no more; neither shall the children of wickedness affect them any more." He urged the eager Puritans to "Go forth ... as the Israelites did," and concluded, "...ever let the name of the Lord be your strong tower, and the word of His promise, the rock of your refuge. His word that made heaven and earth will not fail, till heaven and earth are no more."[4]

On June 12, nearly 400 new Puritan settlers set foot on their Promised Land for the first time. They were dismayed to say the least. John Endecott had been in charge of the struggling colony for nearly two years, and he was glad to surrender to Winthrop's leadership. Of the 268 men who had come to Salem, only 85 remained, and others could not wait to go back on the first ship. Endecott had gone as far as he could go. The colony had survived, but to thrive, it needed a God-sent leader. Winthrop was the man. He wrote the following in his early days at Salem in 1630, concerning the covenant with God.

> "... If the Lord shall please to hear us, and bring us in peace to the place we desire, then hath He ratified this Covenant and sealed our Commission, [and] will expect a strict performance of the Articles contained in it. But if we shall neglect the observance of these Articles ... the Lord will surely break out in wrath against us."[5]

With Winthrop at the helm, the dying colony was revived. When the colony needed wisdom, Winthrop sought the leadership of God and always seemed to do the right thing. When the colony needed finances, the able governor sought the Lord and God always supplied, oftentimes out of Winthrop's own pocket or personal fortune. The governor laid aside his role of the English gentry and happily worked side-by-side with the common laborer to build a new work in a New England. The people rallied to him. Cotton Mather, the Puritan historian, called Winthrop the American Nehemiah.

Several months after his arrival, Governor Winthrop founded the city of Boston, since Salem could no longer accommodate the influx of settlers. He took John Cotton with him, and he became the pastor of the first church there. The colony was to ever be linked civilly and spiritually. The idea was a Biblical Commonwealth – a theocracy, ruled by God through elected individuals who understood their solemn responsibility before God and man. The foundation of this civilization was built upon six reformation truths that are the bedrock of this country to this day:

1. **The Covenant with God** – The Puritans believed that they were bound to a divine covenant with God to live as He directed. Each area of their life was to be lived for the glory of God and others. In the covenant, God is obligated to man and man to God. Winthrop mentions this covenant

relationship with man. "Thus stands the cause between God and us: we are entered into covenant with Him for this work."[6]

2. **The Sovereignty of God** – Every aspect of life should be governed by the Word of God. God has created civil order to perform His will and work, therefore civil authorities are subject to God's Word. This would allow for men to select others to rule over them in the "fear of the Lord."

> "In Puritan political theory the magistrate derived his powers from God and not from the people ... His powers did not come from the people, nor was he primarily responsible to them for the stewardship of his office ... it must never be forgotten that both the voters and the magistrates were to look to the Scriptures as a guide for the general conduct of their government. The rulers and the people were thus subject to the revealed will of God, and the will of the people could never take precedence over the divinely ordained powers and functions of human government."[7]

3. **The Total Depravity of Mankind** – The Puritans saw all men as fallen and in need

of salvation by God's grace. Since all are depraved, there was a need for civil government with limited authority. Since no man could be trusted explicitly, there was also a need for written law.

4. **The Preeminence of the Law of God** – The Word of God was considered the law of the colony. There was no higher law than that of God since there was no higher authority than God. The idea of a theocracy permeated every area of Puritan thought and life.

> "The Church and State were to cooperate in the attainment of their respective goals, for they were both subject to the same God. It was for this reason that the State was to punish blasphemers and heretics. The magistrate, in the discharge of his office, was a steward unto God and he was to be found faithful in this responsibility. It was not the role of the magistrate to proclaim the Gospel, but it was his duty to establish such civil conditions as to enable the Church to perform this function. Neither was it the responsibility of the Church to manage the civil life of the people, but a faithful preaching of the Law of

God was bound to have a healthy influence on the community at large."[8]

5. **The Necessity of the Redemption of Man through God's Grace** – The Puritan view of man is that if left to his own devices, he would be eternally lost. No amount of enlightenment can save him, only the unmerited favor of God. Therefore man must come to the saving grace of God. This was the Puritan mission statement – to bring the lost to Christ.
6. **The Kingdom of God on Earth** – The Puritans foresaw their work actually developing into God's millennium kingdom on Earth. This is the postmillennial view of eschatology. From the persecuted Puritan perspective, a move to the New World would be the logical step of progression to usher in God's Kingdom on the Earth.

From these civil and theological perspectives, the Puritans planted their colonies in the New World. From these colonies would come a new nation conceived in liberty – the same liberties that the Israelites longed for in Egypt and the same freedoms they dreamed of in the Promised Land.

10

Conceived in Liberty

The Puritans could have had no idea of the sense of liberties that they would possess once they set foot in America. In 1630, America was not yet a nation. It was not even much of a colony – just a dream. But it would be a great nation one day, and it all started with a dream – a dream of freedom. Step by step, God led his people to a greater sense of freedom. By providence, the Massachusetts Bay Colony established an independent colony outside of entangling governmental controls by the crown. The charter also called for a type of self-government which the Puritans began to put in place as soon as they arrived in America. One stated goal for coming to America was to establish "a Church State among them, and for making a confession of their faith, and entering into an holy Covenant, whereby that Church State was formed."[1] The Puritan view of religious freedom and civil government was fused together in a theocracy, where God would rule through morally righteous leaders. There was never an idea of a separation of church and state, but they would be one union that could not be dissolved. This can best be seen as the 1641 Massachusetts Body of Liberties prescribed a list of capital crimes based upon the Bible. The first 11 offenses not only carry the death penalty, but also list the Biblical reference for the sentence.

1. "If any man after legal conviction shall have or worship any other god, but the Lord God, he shall be put to death. (Deut. 13:6, 10; 17:2, 6; Ex. 22:20)"
2. "If any man or woman be a witch (that is, has or consults with a familiar spirit), they shall be put to death. (Ex. 22:18; Lev. 20:27; Deut. 18:10)"
3. "If any man shall blaspheme the name of God the Father, Son, or Holy Ghost, with direct, express, presumptuous, or high handed blasphemy, or shall curse God in the like manner, he shall be put to death. (Lev. 25:15, 16)"
4. "If any person commits any willful murder, which is manslaughter, committed upon premeditated malice, hatred, or cruelty, not in a man's necessary and just defense, nor by mere casualty against his will, he shall be put to death. (Ex. 21:12; Num. 35:13, 14, 30, 31)"
5. "If any person slays another suddenly in his anger or cruelty of passion, he shall be put to death. (Num. 35:20, 21; Lev. 24:17)"

6. "If any person shall slay another through guile, either by poisoning or other such devilish practice, he shall be put to death. (Ex. 21:14)"
7. "If any man or woman shall lie with any beast or brute creature by carnal copulation, they shall surely be put to death. And the beast shall be slain and buried, and not eaten. (Lev. 20:15, 16)"
8. "If any man lies with mankind as he lies with a woman, both of them have committed abomination, they both shall surely be put to death. (Lev. 20:13)"
9. "If any person commits adultery with a married or espoused wife, the adulterer and adulteress shall surely be put to death. (Lev. 20:18, 19, 20; Deut. 22:23, 24)"
10. "If any person steals a man or mankind, he shall surely be put to death. (Ex. 21:16)"
11. "If any man rises up by false witness, wittingly and of purpose to take away any man's life, he shall be put to death. (Deut. 19:16, 18, 19)"[2]

The Puritans viewed their freedoms as a result of their personal walk of obedience with their Creator. Their behavior was patterned after examples and instruction from the Bible. Therefore, the two, freedom and responsibility, were directly related. The Puritans came to America for the freedom to not only worship God, but also to live as God directed.

To shirk any responsibility, civil, moral, or religious, would endanger the blessings of God and run the risk of forfeiting precious freedom that their relationship with God provided. This idea does not minimize the grace of God, but illustrates the overall importance of man's covenant with God. Cotton Mather recorded the Puritanical Covenant in this way:

> "We covenant with our Lord, and one with another; and we do bind ourselves in the presence of God, to walk together in all his ways, according as he pleased to reveal himself unto us in his blessed word of truth; and do explicitly, in the name and fear of God, profess and protest to walk as followeth, through the power and grace of our Lord Jesus Christ."[3]

The covenant included vertical as well as horizontal relationships. One's primary relationship was toward God, but also included the fellowship of believers. The "binding" together would include the Christian brotherhood, while "walk" meant the Christian lifestyle. The guide, whether civil, moral, or religious, was to be "His blessed word of truth." The power for living in the wilderness of the American frontier would be the wonderful "grace of our Lord Jesus Christ." The early Puritan was fully supplied. Armed with this covenant, he could withstand severe winters, savage Indian attacks and survive any opposition of the wicked one.

As Puritan life developed in New England, so did the concept of the Covenant. In 1648, church leaders met at Cambridge, Massachusetts and developed a manual for American church discipline, *The Synodicom Americanum*. This manual expressed thoroughly their Christian beliefs as to life and ministry in the colony.

> God, the supreme Lord and King of all the world, hath ordained civil magistrates to be under him, over the people for his own glory and the public good: And to this end has armed them with the power of the sword for the defense and encouragement of them that do good, and for the punishment of evil doers.
>
> It is lawful for Christians to accept and execute the office of a magistrate, when called thereunto: In the management whereof, as they ought especially to maintain piety, justice and peace, according to the wholesome laws of each common-wealth, so for that end, they may lawfully now under the New Testament wage war upon just and necessary occasion.[4]

This manual, the first of its kind in America, stressed the ultimate authority was God. That authority was handed down to religious and civil authorities. Since power, authority and direction is vested in the written word, the Puritans thought it logical and necessary to follow His pattern and order their society by written law. This was unique, since their English homeland had no written constitution.

British common law was mainly oral tradition, cited in various written court decisions. The first written code of laws was the Massachusetts Body of Liberties in 1641. The Bible was central to this initial document, as was almost every law of the early Puritan colonies.

In 1634, settlers from Plymouth started a new community at Wethersfield, Connecticut. Two years later, Reverend Thomas Hooker led about 100 Puritans from Massachusetts to establish a new model community at Hartford, Connecticut. Hooker was a Puritan minister who fled England for Holland to avoid investigation. He arrived in the New World in 1633. Due to his disagreement with the structure of Puritan government, he peacefully left Massachusetts for Connecticut. The latter was settled by people who had freely chosen to leave, not as disgruntled financiers, but as people who believed in responsible self-government. For his work, Hooker is referred to as the "Father of American Democracy."

His powerful preaching provided a foundation for the Fundamental Orders of Connecticut. Drafted in 1639, this was the first written constitution in the history of the world. The following is that constitution's preamble:

> "Forasmuch as it has pleased Almighty God by the wise disposition of His Divine Providence so to order and dispose of things that we the inhabitants and residents of Windsor, Hartford, and Wethersfield and now cohabiting and dwelling in and upon the river

Conectocotte [Connecticut] and the lands thereunto adjoining; and well knowing where a people are gathered together the Word of God requires that to maintain the peace and union of such a people there should be an orderly and decent government established according to God, to order and dispose of the affairs of all the people at all seasons as occasions shall require; do therefore associate and conjoin ourselves to be as one public State or Commonwealth, and do, for ourselves and our successors and such as shall be adjoined to us at any time hereafter, enter into combination and confederation together, to maintain and preserve the liberty and purity of the Gospel of our Lord Jesus which we now profess, as also the discipline of the churches, which according to the truth of the said Gospel is now practiced among us."[5]

John Fiske, in his 1889 *Beginnings of New England,* cites Hooker's sermon and speculates that it was ideas like Hooker's that gave rise to America's national government.

[He] preached a sermon of wonderful power, in which he maintained that 'the foundation of authority is laid in the free consent of the people, that the choice of public magistrates belongs unto the people by God's own allowance,' and that 'they who have power to appoint officers and magistrates have the right also to set the bounds and limitations of the power and place unto which they call them.'[6]

The present-day government of the United States is more closely related to that of Connecticut than to any of the other 12 colonies.

The Puritan concept of relationship to God and responsibility before Him had, and still has, a profound bearing on America. From this perspective, the English Purists conceived a new type of government on a new continent – a government and a land far removed from the encroachment of royal tyrants or religious hierarchy. In the Puritan mind, if that new order in a New England was given time, it might develop far beyond their wildest imaginations. Author and attorney John Gibbs, Jr. stated the following of the Puritans:

> It was both their theological and political practices, as well as their written agreements for self-government based on the Bible, that have had the greatest impact on America … the Puritan practice of church covenants gave rise to the concept of political covenants, compacts, and written constitutions. Ultimately, these documents did much to inspire the United States Constitution, which survives to this day.[7]

11

The Most Misunderstood Man in America

When the English ship, *The Lyon,* arrived in Boston Harbor in 1631, the Massachusetts Colony was barely three years old, and the ancient town of Plymouth not yet in its teens. The ink was barely dry on the unique Bay Colony's patent granted by Charles I in 1629. The inaugural year of Massachusetts had been an exciting one. Governor John Endecott had barely held his starving colony together through the first winter. When other colonists arrived in 1629, things looked bleak, but worsened during the winter. In 1630, Governor John Winthrop relieved Endecott to find only 85 survivors of the colony. Due to Winthrop's meticulous organizational skills and boundless enthusiasm, the settlement began to thrive. By the next year, a second town, Boston, was established to prepare for the rapid development of the colony as a whole.

It was in these bright and optimistic days that Roger Williams set foot on Puritan New England's soil. Williams was 28, married, and a Puritan minister who had chosen to be a private family chaplain rather than an Anglican priest, following his graduation from Cambridge. He was extremely disillusioned with the Church of England and sought a new life and ministry in the lands of America.

> Upon his arrival in Massachusetts, Roger Williams discovered at once that the New World was not new enough — and the Puritans he found there not pure enough — to satisfy his demanding conscience.[1]

Immediately, Governor Winthrop offered Williams the prestigious opportunity to be the teacher at the Boston church. Since the pulpit was temporarily vacant, this would have given Williams the position of interim pastor. He flatly refused the offer and also refused to take communion with the Puritan Christians of Boston, because they had not broken fellowship with the powerful Church of England.

Having alienated himself from the Bostonians, Williams moved to Salem, which held stronger separatist tendencies. The Salem Church was without a teacher, and initially offered the position to the winsome and fiery young Williams. Massachusetts authorities had a different opinion of the English upstart. Without a trial, Williams was unofficially tried and found to be too independent for the Salem Church.

He responded by relocating to Plymouth, the citadel of separatism in America. The Pilgrim experience only lasted two years and abruptly ended when the Pilgrims failed to be the Separatists that Williams thought they should be. When returning to the Mother Country, some Pilgrims would worship with Anglican friends in their hosts' churches. This violated Roger Williams's sense of second degree separation. Not only would he separate from the Church of England, but he also required those with whom he fellowshipped to be separate as well. He cut his ties with Plymouth and returned to Salem and accepted the pastorate of the Puritan Congregational Church in the town.

Before long, trouble was evident. Williams called for complete separation from the Church of England, and then began talk of separating from England itself. His basis for his disillusionment was that the King of England had no right to give the Massachusetts Colony the lands which so obviously belonged to the Indians. He encouraged the colony to return its patent to the king and purchase the territory from its rightful native owners. Even though the Salem Puritans had drifted far from their Anglican Mother Church, they had gone as far as they desired to go. Years of perseverance to correct the errors of Anglicanism had only frustrated the purists. As a last resort, they had not left the church, only the continent. In theory, they were still English and still Anglican. Their cherished covenant called for the Creator alone to guide them while they enjoyed the freedoms of Puritan Anglicanism just outside the grasp of the tyrannical Bishop Laud in London. By providence, God had allowed the Massachusetts Bay Colony charter, issued by King Charles, to allow the colony to operate separate from suppressive English control. The Puritan New Englanders could not afford to lose any of their precious freedoms that the charter granted. Therefore, neither king nor bishop could be alienated. The colony could be separate in theory, but attached in both religious and civil authority. This, Roger Williams did not understand or accept. He owed only allegiance to God, not to man. Since he viewed both King Charles and his henchman, Laud, as heretical, he sought to separate.

In April of 1634, the Massachusetts magistrates ordered all adult males of the colony to take an oath of loyalty or be banished. Williams rejected the ordinance and openly opposed it. The leadership of the colony took every measure possible to deal with the boisterous Salem pastor.

> It appears that, of all those who tried to argue and plead with him (and that included at different times Thomas Hooker, John Cotton, William Bradford, and Edward Winslow) John Winthrop came the closest to reaching his heart. In fact, Williams may well have considered the compassionate Governor his closest personal friend throughout the remainder of his life. But when it came to a matter of principle, he would never permit himself to back down. Besides, as much as he might have been tempted by Winthrop's vision, the covenanted kingdom which Winthrop was describing cut across the principle which Williams held to be the dearest of

all: *liberty of conscience* ('Nobody is going to tell me what I should do or believe.').[2]

All efforts failed. The unbending Williams could not compromise on what the New Englanders considered to be a providential blessing of God – their 1629 patent or charter. Governor Winthrop viewed the life of his infant colony at risk when he called for the trial of Roger Williams. In September 1635, the General Court of Massachusetts banished the maverick Williams by stating the following:

"Whereas Mr. Roger Williams, one of the elders of the church of Salem, has broached and divulged divers new and dangerous opinions, against the authority of magistrates, has also wrote letters of defamation, both of the magistrates and churches here, and that before any conviction, and yet maintains the same without retraction, it is therefore ordered, that the said Mr. Williams shall depart out of this jurisdiction within six weeks now next ensuing, which if he neglect to perform, it shall be lawful for the Governor and two of the magistrates to send him to some place out of this jurisdiction, not to return any more without license from the Court."[3]

Even though the sentence stated that Williams had 60 days to depart the colony, he took longer, and undoubtedly the Puritan governor would have given him until the spring of 1636 if he would have bridled his tongue. But, he did not. He could not be quiet on the issues that mattered so much to him. Puritan leaders felt they had no recourse but to forcibly send the overzealous preacher back to the jurisdiction of the English Church, his native soil from whence he came in 1631. When Williams heard of the plot to extradite him, he fled to the wilderness that became Rhode Island, rather than be shipped forcibly back to England.[4]

The exiled preacher departed in the bitter cold of the New England winter. He found refuge with Indians whom he had previously befriended. In the spring, he was joined by four men who started a settlement across the Narragansett Bay, which they called Providence. They purchased land from the Indians and began missionary efforts to evangelize the tribes of the region. This may well have been Williams's most fruitful ministry. As a result, Rhode Island was the only colony in the Americas that escaped Indian massacres. Due to his carefully cultivated friendship with the Narragansett tribe, Williams was able to provide Governor Winthrop with valuable information that saved the Massachusetts colony from several savage Indian attacks.[5]

The weary Williams was a family church chaplain rather than a practicing Anglican in England. In America, he was a reluctant missionary to the Indians, rather than returning to his homeland. He was a preacher without a parish. Who was this purest of all Puritans? Roger Williams appears to be the enigma of his day. Some historians glorify him, while others demonize him. There is no doubt he was colorful, controversial and charismatic. Note what Steven Wilkins says about him:

> To modern twentieth century Americans, Roger Williams is the one 'shining light' in the midst of that whole sorry 'darkness' which was the Puritan era in this country. According to the accepted story, the Puritans were extremely intolerant folk, paranoid of anyone who didn't believe precisely as they, and utterly unwilling to consider differing views. Because of this, they cast out Roger Williams (that gracious, sweet-spirited man who only desired religious liberty). He was banished from Massachusetts Bay, merely because he was a Baptist and forced to flee from his persecutors by making a heroic escape into a harsh, New England winter.[6]

Marshall and Manuel are in agreement with Wilkins as to the character of Roger Williams.

> Roger Williams was the most tragic and intriguing of all zealous Christians: a purist. 'Charming, sweet-tempered, winning, courageous, selfless, God-intoxicated and stubborn,' he was so obsessed with being doctrinally and ecclesiastically pure that not even the Puritans were pure enough for him. From the moment he stepped off the boat, he brought anguish to the hearts of all who came to know him. Because to know him was to

like him, no matter how impossible were the tenets he insisted upon.

Williams' insistence upon absolute purity in the Church, beyond all normal extremes, grew out of his own personal obsessions with having to be right — in doctrine, in conduct, in church associations — in short, in every area of life. This need to be right colored everything he did or thought; indeed, it drove him into one untenable position after another.[7]

In contrast to contemporary historians, Richard B. Cook writes in 1891:

Roger Williams was driven from the colony of Massachusetts because of his Baptist principle, and became the founder of the state of Rhode Island. He was accused of preaching against the assumption of power in the religious affairs by the civil magistrate, and besides was charged with holding other views tending to Anabaptist. He was tried by the court and sentenced to be banished. He fled the cruelties of his Christian brethren, to find refuge and hospitality among the savages of the forest.[8]

William Grady in *What Hath God Wrought* places fault with the Puritans in the Williams banishment:

And so, in the dead winter, Roger Williams, accompanied by a small band of loyal parishioners, entered what he would later describe as a 'miserable, cold, howling wilderness,' without either *bed, bread,* or *lead.* Fortunately for all, Williams had been a faithful witness to the Indians while sojourning with the Pilgrims.[9]

The Puritan Cotton Mather provides us with his observations of Roger Williams in the book *Magnolia Christi Americana*:

> About the year 1630, arrived here one Mr. Roger Williams; who being a preacher that had less light than fire in him, hath by his own sad example, preached unto us the danger of that evil which the apostle mentions in Romans 10:2 – 'They have a zeal, but not according to knowledge.'[10]

Without a doubt, Williams was a Separatist. His sect went far beyond the views of the Puritans, who merely sought to purify the Anglican Church. Williams was more at home with the Pilgrims who came out of the Church of England than the Puritans. His greatest ministry in Massachusetts was at Plymouth. His reason for leaving that pastorate was separation. This he emphatically practiced. He separated from the Church of England and then from the purists in the Congregational Church in Massachusetts. He proceeded to separate from the Separatist Pilgrims to go back to the Puritans, whom he denounced and from which he was banished. Upon separating from the Massachusetts Colony, he worshipped with those who came to Providence. When contacted by Baptist doctrine, he became a Baptist, but separated on the grounds that there was no clearly defined line of apostolic succession to the Baptist Church.[11] This radical separation led Williams to abandon any hope of finding a pure church on Earth.

In time, others would follow the Williams example of separation and join him at Providence. Later, the tiny settlement grew into a tiny colony of several settlements and eventually Rhode Island was born. It is with the founding of this new colony that we see the paradox in Roger Williams. He sailed to London to procure a Royal Charter from King Charles for his new adventure. And what an adventure it was!

> "Populated at first by those who had remained loyal to him at Salem, Providence now became a magnet for every crackpot, rebel, misfit, and independent on the Atlantic seaboard. And he, as president, was responsible for keeping order. What a nightmare!"[12]

Ironically it was his lack of toleration that placed him outside the Puritan New Israel, but it was his love for toleration that helped him establish a haven for religious refugees in the New World. Williams was unable to tolerate the apostasy of Anglicanism. He refused infant baptism and embraced the ideals of English Baptists, at least for a while. Williams also refuted the Puritan idea of an ecclesiastical civil court. He preached "soul liberty" – you cannot force a person to comply with civil law in a spiritual way. In reality, Williams separated from the Anglican Church, then from the Puritan civilization and later from his Baptist beliefs into a separated life where he only took communion with his wife.[13] Who understood Roger Williams? John Quincy Adams referred to him as "altogether revolutionary." This may be the best analysis of the founder of Rhode Island. America's first revolutionary, but more than a harbinger of war, Williams was a man of peace as well. His religious tolerance became a model for the American way of life once America earned its independence. Williams's separatists views were correct – civilly and religiously. But the Puritan leaders of 1635 were equally correct in thinking that Williams's ideas would birth a premature American revolt, a revolt that would strangle an infant nation in its cradle. Both being right, both Williams and the Puritans must wait for God's timing to "bring forth a new nation conceived in liberty and dedicated to the proposition that all men are created equal." Only time would reveal Roger Williams's banishment as a way to form a model of religious liberty in Rhode Island. Only time would show that the Puritan banishment helped to begin a viable religion in American life.

12

The Rise of Other Colonies in America

New Netherlands

The settlement of New York is different than any other in America. When Henry Hudson explored the river which bears his name in 1609, he claimed the area for Holland, since he was employed by a Dutch trading company. Since the Pilgrims left from Holland bound for this part of the New World, it is thought by some that the Dutch bribed the shipmaster of the *Mayflower* to lead them astray. The idea was that one day the Dutch would eventually settle in the rich Hudson River Valley and control its port and waterway. Whether this is truth or fable, no one will ever know. However, four years after the Pilgrims settled in Plymouth, the Dutch with 30 families arrived in their "New Netherlands" on the Hudson. Most of these were hard-working, thrifty Protestant refugees from the Southern Netherlands. They purchased Manhattan Island from the Indians and quickly went to work on farming and housing. Since most of the early settlers were an amalgamation of Protestants, religion was with liberty in the Dutch colony, constrained only by the term "reformed religion" in the 1621 Dutch West India Charter.

> [The colonists] shall practise no other form of divine worship within their territory than that of the Reformed religion as presently practised here in this country, and, in so doing, by their Christian life and conduct, lead the Indians and other blind people to the knowledge of God and of His Word, without, however, persecuting anyone because of his faith, but leaving everyone the freedom of his conscience. But, if anyone among them or within their jurisdiction should wantonly revile or blaspheme the name of God or of our Savior Jesus Christ, he shall be punished by the commander and his council according to the circumstances.

> *Whereas* a considerable number of respectable Englishmen, with their clergyman, have applied to us for permission to settle here and to reside under us, and requested that some articles might be offered to them, we have therefore resolved to communicate the following articles to them:
>
> 1. They shall be bound to take the oath of allegiance to the Noble

> Lords States General and the East India Company, under whose protection they shall reside.
> 2. They shall enjoy free exercise of religion.[1]

The first 40 years of existence were years of external strife. The British contested the claims of Hudson since John Cabot's exploration predated that of Hudson. In 1664, the Dutch permanently surrendered control of their foothold in America, but remained as part of the fabric of its culture. When the English took over this colony, which they renamed New York, the Church of England became the established church in New York. In 1665, the colonial legislature passed the following bill to enable religion to thrive in the colony.

> It is ordered that a church shall be built in each parish, capable of holding two hundred persons; that ministers of every church shall preach every Sunday, and pray for the king, queen, the Duke of York, and the royal family; and to marry persons after legal publication of license.[2]

In 1673, each town was authorized to enact laws that would protect the Sabbath and guard against Sabbath breaking.

Delaware and New Jersey

New Sweden, as Delaware was first referred to, was settled by the Swedes in 1638. A trade conflict with the Dutch of New Netherlands evoked a small war, in which the Swedes surrendered without a shot. Delaware was annexed by the victors and the Swedes eventually melted into the Dutch-English society of the region. The history of New Jersey is much the same as Delaware and New York. Part of the region was sold to Quakers in the late 1600s, leaving it a melting pot of customs, societies and religion. The 1677 Charter of West New Jersey vaguely states the freedom of religion in the colony.

> That no men nor number of men upon earth have power or authority to rule over men's consciences in religious matters ... But that all and every such person and persons may, from time to time, and at all times, freely and fully have and enjoy his and their judgments, and the exercises of their consciences in matters of religious worship throughout all the said Province.[3]

New Hampshire

The initial settlements in New Hampshire were independent ventures begun by adventurers and enterprising settlers who sought economic gain. These pioneers found themselves unable to defend their small colony from Indian attacks. Therefore, they united with the Massachusetts colony in 1641. This union continued for 38 years, at which time New Hampshire became a separate governing province. The 1679 Provincial Papers of the region state the following:

> And, above all things we do by these presents, will, require, and command our said Council, to take all possible care for the discountenancing of vice, and encouraging of virtue and good living; and that by such examples, the infidel may be incited and desire to partake of the Christian religion; and for the greater ease and satisfaction of the said loving subjects in matters of religion, we do hereby require and command that liberty of conscience shall be allowed unto all Protestants.[4]

A law was passed to protect Christianity from those who might "willfully presume to blaspheme the holy name of God the Father, Son and Holy Ghost, with direct, express, presumptuous or high-handed blasphemy, either by willful or obstinate denying the true God, or his creation, or government of the world."[5]

Maryland

Lord Baltimore arrived in America in 1634, and established a settlement of the St. George River,

Maryland. There were two motives for founding a new colony in this area. The first was to establish a haven for Catholics. Even though Anglicanism was the official religion of England, Catholicism was still well recognized. They viewed America as a way of exercising their freedom to worship God. Secondly, Maryland provided a way to build a large estate for Lord Baltimore. In order to provide liberty to the Catholics and still entice Protestants, the colony's leadership passed a religious Toleration Act in 1649. This legislation provided that no one professing a belief in Christ should be forbidden to freely exercise his religion. In reality, the idea was that of protecting Catholics while inviting Protestants. This act worked in favor of the Protestants. By the time of the War of Independence, only one percent of Maryland's population was Catholic. Later, this type of religious toleration became part of the entire American way of life. Excerpts from the Maryland Toleration Act are given below:

> Forasmuch as in a well-governed and Christian commonwealth, matters concerning religion and the honor of God ought in the first place to be taken into serious consideration and endeavored to be settled, *be it therefore ordered and enacted,* ... that whatsoever person or persons within this province ... shall henceforth blaspheme God, curse Him, or deny our Savior Jesus Christ to be the Son of God, or shall deny the Holy Trinity - ... or the Godhead ... or shall use or utter

any reproachful speeches, words, or language concerning the said Holy Trinity, … shall be punished with death and confiscation or forfeiture of all his or her lands and goods to the Lord Proprietary and his heirs.[6]

Rhode Island

The tiny state of Rhode Island was settled primarily by Puritan colonists who left Massachusetts, the first of which was Roger Williams, who came to Cape Cod in 1630. Initially, Williams was received by the Salem Church with open arms, but as time progressed, the relationship with Williams disintegrated. He openly criticized the church and called for separation from the Mother Church in England. So violent was Williams in his opposition to the state religion of Massachusetts that even his friend and defender, Governor John Winthrop, advised him to leave the colony. This he did in 1636, while naming his new settlement Providence, because God's hand of protection had been upon his departure from the Bay Colony.

In 1638, Anne Hutchinson, along with a small band of followers, settled in Rhode Island. She, too, was critical of Puritan teachings. "In prayer meetings in her home, she began to teach that outward obedience and behavior were not important and that the Bible was not God's final revelation."[7] She and her followers became known as "Antinomians" (against law), since they did not believe that a Christian should be required to live by Biblical standards of behavior. She, like Williams, was expelled from the Puritan colony, but given several months to relocate her residence.

A physician, John Clarke, was part of the Hutchinson departure from Massachusetts in 1638. He, along with William Harris, founded the first Baptist Church in Rhode Island. Murray Rothbard, in *Conceived in Liberty,* notes that Roger Williams temporarily converted "to the Baptist faith in early 1639. The inveterate Baptist insistence on individual conscience and the right of religious liberty was very close to Williams's views. In addition, each Baptist church was separate and completely autonomous: The officers are democratically elected by the entire congregation. In a few months, however, Williams shifted again to become a Seeker."[8] In spite of the loss of Roger Williams, the Baptists had a foothold in America that would remain strong until today, and the civil liberties which both have espoused have become a hallmark of American life.

The Carolinas

The Carolinas were populated by several different groups of settlers. Some 65 years after the ill-fated Roanoke settlement, Virginians began to make their way into the northern section of the Carolinas. They founded Albemarle on a sound off the Atlantic Ocean. The leader of this first settlement was Roger Green, a Presbyterian minister. In 1663, King Charles II granted a proprietary charter to eight of his chosen courtiers. The grant included the territory from southern Virginia to the Spanish claim in Florida. To solicit settlers, the proprietors granted religious freedom to all who would relocate to their Carolina venture. The Anglican Church became the established church, but Quakers, Baptists, Presbyterians, and Congregationalists outnumbered the Anglicans in this southern colony. The seventeenth century religious fervor did not affect Carolina as it did the other colonies. The Quaker, George Fox, visited Albemarle in 1672 and wrote of no place to worship in the entire city. William Byrd, a wealthy Virginia planter who traveled south, noted, "This is the only metropolis in the Christian or Mohammedan world where there is neither church, chapel, mosque, synagogue or any other place of public worship of any sect of religion."[9] The early Carolinians were free to worship as they saw fit. Most must have invoked God's blessings in a private or family setting.

Pennsylvania

Charles II, the British monarch, owed a large debt to the Penn family. To retire that debt, he granted William Penn a Royal Charter in 1681 to include the territory between Maryland and New York. This gave Penn a sole proprietorship to the colony. He immediately sought to make this region of America a haven for his Society of Friends. The Quakers, as they were called, were unique in several of their religious and secular beliefs. They opposed war in an age when war was glorified. The sect was very pious in their beliefs, but held to the teaching that man is led by an "inner light," independent from the Word of God. This "inner light" would guide man to accomplish good works which earned him eternal reward. This unique type of religion made the Friends very tolerant of other religious groups. They opened their settlement to many German Protestants, such as the Amish, the Moravians, and the Mennonites.

The initial legislative act of Pennsylvania was enacted in December of 1682.

> 'Whereas the glory of Almighty God and the good of Mankind, is the reason and end of government, and therefore, government in itself is a venerable Ordinance of God,' therefore, it is the purpose of civil government to 'establish such laws as shall best preserve true Christian and Civil Liberty, in opposition to all Unchristian, Licentious, and unjust practices, (Whereby God may have his due, and Caesar his due, and the people their due), from tyranny and oppression ...'[10]

When establishing a form of government, William Penn surrendered all personal power as the sole proprietor of the colony. He set up a colony with civil and religious liberties ensured by written law. He refused to be a tyrant that ruled with a capricious iron fist. Religion and government were to be inseparable in Pennsylvania. David Gibbs says this of the founders:

> It is very clear that what Penn envisioned for his colony was not freedom *from* religion, but freedom *of* religion – not a separation of government from all religion, but a government that respected the religious consciences of all its citizens. He envisioned a place where every man was free, not to live an ungodly life, but to practice his own religion in peace, to have the right to rule his own estate, and to participate in making laws and enforcing them. Individual freedom could only work if the people were self-governed and industrious.[11]

Georgia

General James Oglethorpe developed a plan to provide a safe haven for persecuted Christians and underprivileged citizens of England. On June 9, 1732, he was granted a royal charter by George II to establish a new colony near the Spanish claim in Florida. This was the only British colony that was subsidized by Parliament. Though Oglethorpe's reason for founding a colony may have been religious, Parliament's reasons were secular. First, a vast amount of the early Georgian settlers were from the English lower class. The second reason was to establish a buffer between the Spanish territory of

Florida and the "respectable" English colony of the Carolinas. The primary charter granted each settler 50 acres to settle in the region, and more if they paid their own passage to America. Oglethorpe supplied farm implements to work the fields and encouraged the settlers to be industrious and self-disciplined.

> By the charter, the proprietors were a group of twenty-one trustees — the Georgia Trust — none of whom was to be allowed to reap personal gain or profit from the colony. The Trust was to run the colony for twenty-one years, after which the land would revert to the Crown. All laws of Georgia were to be subject to the king's approval. Religious freedom was to be enjoyed in the colony by all except Catholics, who apparently did not come under any sort of 'humanitarian' jurisdiction … From its very inception, here was the only colony where the citizens had no representative assembly whatever and, indeed, little say over their own lives and actions.[12]

13

The Salem Witch Trials

For a nine-month period in 1692, hysteria and spiritual wickedness reigned over godliness and common law, in and around Puritan Salem, Massachusetts. The seeds of spiritual darkness had been sown years before. Cotton Mather noted this as well as William Bradford. In essence, these contemporaries had bewailed the spiritual decline in Puritanism. At Salem, ministers stayed only briefly at the second oldest parish in the colony. Bitterness and strife were noted mainly in the Putnam and Porter clans. These families had feuded for years after bringing civil suits against each other in violation of Scripture. Therefore, Salem was a natural place for spiritual warfare to break out. But the first shot was fired in a very unusual location – the basement of the parsonage. The Pastor, Samuel Paris, had brought with him to Salem an Indian servant named "Tittuba" from Barbados. Unbeknownst to the Parises, elements of Voodoo and witchcraft were in the basement. The practices quickly spread to other girls of the community. Soon, bizarre occurrences were noted in town. Documentation by reliable sources indicates various inexplicable happenings: 1) Girls seeing things that no one else saw. 2) Supernatural afflictions upon the girls such as teeth marks, punch marks, etc. 3) The girls being miraculously thrown around. 4) Levitations of the girls supernaturally. 5) Ghost-like beings that were of identifiable persons. 6) Open arguments by the girls with the preacher during church services.

As the hysteria built, the parents, pastors, town and church all seemed powerless to stop the phenomena. Eventually, the seven girls, ages 9 to 20, accused over 100 people of being witches. Most of those accused were social enemies of their parents. Many of the accused were strong Christian pillars of both the church and the community. No one was above the accusation of witchcraft. The town was at the mercy and whim of the band of occult-dabbling adolescents. When the trials commenced, Massachusetts clergymen called for common law to be practiced and spiritual mindedness to reign. Neither was practiced. Note Cotton Mather's plea for due process of law in *Magnolia Christi Americana*:

> They [the area ministers] now say, that the more the afflicted were harkened unto, the more the number of the accused increased; until at last many scores were cried out upon, and among them, some who, by the unblameableness – yea, and serviceableness – of their whole conversation, had obtained the just

reputation of good people among all that were acquainted with them. The character of the afflicted likewise added unto the common distaste; for though some of them too were good people, yet others of them, and such of them as were most flippant at accusing, had a far other character.[1]

There is no apparent practice of common law during the trials. The basic rudiments of law were ignored. First, the court woefully violated the principle that the accused is innocent until proven guilty. Their guilt was assumed the moment that they were accused.

The judge's questioning also reveals their attitude. Prisoners were not asked whether they tormented the afflicted, but why and how they did so. Mrs. Nathaniel Cary was ordered to stand with her arms outstretched, to prevent her from inflicting sympathetic harm. When Cary asked permission to support his wife, he was told that if she had strength to torment the afflicted, she had strength to stand by herself.[2]

Secondly, the court allowed what they called "spectral evidence." That is, if one accused another of being a witch based upon seeing his or her "specter" (ghost), that testimony was admissible, even though the ghost was only seen by the accuser. This evidence, though startling, would not be admitted in another court in the land.

Thirdly, the Puritan court had no Scriptural basis for dealing with witchcraft. Even though the Bible speaks of witchcraft being a capital offense, it provides little basis for discerning witchcraft. Also, the practice is almost impossible to criminally investigate, detect, and try by law.

The fourth error was that the court willfully violated Scripture in allowing a single accuser to supply the only witness against the accused. Numbers 35:30 says, "But one witness shall not testify against any person to cause him to die." Deuteronomy 17:6 states, "At the mouth of two witnesses, or three witnesses shall he that is worthy of death be put to death, but at the mouth of one witness he shall not be put to death." Also in Deuteronomy 19:15 we read, "One witness shall not rise up against a man for any iniquity, or for any sin, in any sin that he sinneth, at the mouth of two witnesses, or at the mouth of three witnesses, shall the matter be established." The court repeatedly accepted dreams and visions that only one person had witnessed.

Lastly, the court would try and convict an accused, and then ask for a confession before the death sentence was executed. There are records that up to 50 people confessed their guilt. For certain, most of these confessions were coerced and others may have been motivated by self-interest, since confessors were not executed.

The question still remains – why the hysteria? There were unexplainable occurrences that happened.

Cotton Mather, who lived during the era, calls it a time of Satanic oppression. The Bible indicates that Satan does have power. Although none of the manifestations that were evident at Salem are present in Scripture, undoubtedly, there was a presence of the occult in Salem.

> Although these diabolical divinations are more ordinarily committed perhaps all over the whole world than they are in the country of New England, yet, that being a country devoted unto the worship and service of the Lord Jesus Christ above the rest of the world, he signalized his vengeance against these wickednesses, with such extraordinary dispensations as have not been often seen in other places.[3]

Even though there are many accounts of prayer and fasting, the Puritan court seemed to act without proper respect for law or Scripture. It appears that God allowed these occurrences as a chastisement upon His people as a warning to repent.

The result of the hysteria and the Salem Witch Trials was not the wholesale execution of hindered and innocent people as one might imagine. No one was burned at the stake, though this was the case in Europe at the same time. Salem did bring its accused to trial. In Europe, thousands were executed without due process of law. At Salem, only 23 people died as a direct result of the trials. Nineteen women were hung, one man was pressed to death and three died in prison. Ironically, Giles Corey, who died with his executioners placing stones upon his chest, had the solution for the problem – submit the girls (his accusers) to their parents for a strong switching. He died unfairly accused, improperly tried, and unscripturally executed, and did not confess that he had ever been a witch.

Four years after the hysteria subsided, Samuel Sewall, a judge in the trials, submitted a public confession and repentance before his church congregation. Twelve jurymen also signed a statement confessing their sin of shedding innocent blood, though it was done "ignorantly and unwittingly." Fourteen years after the trials and executions, one of the key witnesses, Ann Putnam, who accused more than the others, stood before the Salem church to ask for forgiveness of her sins. She stated that she was deceived by Satan and those who died due to her accusations were innocent. In 1706, the Salem church pardoned her and restored her to membership because of her sincere repentance.

14

Missions in America

From the onset, missions and evangelism have been the driving force behind exploration. Columbus declared this as his mission in life – to fulfill the prophecies of his parents who named him the "Christ-bearer." He reinforced it by carrying Christian – Jewish conversers with him to carry the Gospel. Even though Columbus brought the gospel to the Americas, he never realized his goal of evangelizing the masses here. He also never realized his primary goal of liberating the Holy Land and evangelizing Palestine.

The Spanish carried priests with them to the New World, and left behind a legacy of Roman Catholicism. It appears, as one historian noted, that the Spaniards did "little more than sprinkle holy water" on the lost natives of America.

The seventeenth century British marketed their colonization efforts as an avenue to reach to the regions beyond for the glory of God. Captain John Davys, an English naval explorer, supposedly sought for the northwest passage in an effort to better evangelize the world. Richard Hakluyt promoted English exploration as a way to spread the Gospel to the world's heathen and affect the power of the Catholic Church. It is said that Thomas Harriot of Sir Walter Raleigh's Roanoke settlement had a ministry to the Indians, and the Jamestown settlement may have had an impact on evangelizing a few natives.

But by 1630, little had been done to reach the "heathen in America." The Spanish had become too consumed with supplying the homeland with golden tobacco. Marshall and Manuel summarize the missionary endeavors of the first 130 years of American history this way:

> Why had so much gone so wrong in Virginia, when at least the publicly stated motives back in England had been so right? (And so convincing that the Partners themselves had begun to believe them?) The answer is, that in an age and country where practically all the leaders acknowledged God's existence and thereby considered themselves good Christian gentlemen and ladies, hardly anyone was actually living the life Christ calls us to in His Gospel. Even among the ministered, who ere extolling the need for the thrust of Christianity into heathen lands, hardly any were actually prepared to go themselves.
>
> What happened at Jamestown is a horror that we today would like to turn away from

— but if we do, we will lose the whole point ... The settlement of Jamestown was undertaken without Christ. But the next settlers to cross the Atlantic knew better than to attempt it without Him. They knew that they had no choice but to put *all* their trust in Him ...[1]

The Pilgrims and Puritans of New England were a different lot, They came to America for an entirely different reason than the Jamestown settlers. They came for truly religious reasons. They came not just for freedom of religion, but also for freedom from vice and false religion, and the freedom to share the Gospel with other inhabitants, the Native American Indians. The Pilgrims wasted no time in befriending the natives and evangelizing them. The first noteworthy Puritan to conduct missionary work with the Indians was Roger Williams. He learned the language of the Wampanoag while staying with the Pilgrims. Williams had a true love and respect for the Native Americans. He spent months in their villages, teaching them the Bible and sharing the Gospel.

John Elliot, the apostle to the Indians, had the most impressive missionary work among the natives of New England. He translated the Bible into the Algonquin language, pastored a church in Roxbury, Massachusetts and traveled as much as 70 miles each week to preach to the Indians. By 1680, God had used Elliot to establish 14 towns and see over 1,100 natives come to Christ. His converts, called "Praying Indians," were influential in minimizing Indian revolts against the settlers, as well as squelching King Philip's War of 1676.

Thomas Mayhew, Jr. began mission works with the Indians of Nantucket Island in 1646. In a decade, he witnessed nearly 280 converts. When he perished at sea, his father, Thomas Mayhew, Sr., took up the torch of evangelism, and by 1670 had over 3,000 Indian converts who professed Christ as their Savior. By 1700, it is estimated that 7,000 New England Indians had come to Christianity through the ministry of four generations of the Mayhew family. Many of these Indians moved west, carrying the Gospel with them. Missionaries like David Brainerd gave their lives in an effort to reach the Native Americans and help fulfill the Puritan dream to evangelize the lost inhabitants of the New World.

William Penn is another shining example as to his treatment of the Indians. When fur traders offered him 6,000 pounds plus annual royalties for a monopoly to trade with the Delaware and Susquehannah tribes in Pennsylvania, he flatly declined the offer.

> "I will not abuse the love of God ... nor act unworthy of his Providence, by defiling what came to me clean. No; let the Lord guide me by his wisdom to honor his name and serve his truth and people, that an example and a standard may be set up to the nations."[2]

He was known to purchase land from the Indians and treat them with dignity and Christian care. He negotiated a treaty with the Shackamaxon tribe that lasted for nearly 70 years. Penn thought it his Christian duty to treat the Indians fairly and have a part in their evangelization.

One of the avenues in reaching the Native Americans was to supply trained missionaries, pastors, and teachers for the wilderness tribes. The College of William and Mary was established in 1693 at Williamsburg, Virginia for the purpose of a "seminary of ministers of the gospel, and that the youth may be piously educated in good manners and that the Christian faith may be propagated amongst the western Indians to the glory of almighty God."[3] Dartmouth University, which was founded as Moor's Indian Charity School, was founded to teach and train ministers and missionaries to the Indians. The first Europeans may have stumbled carrying the gospel to the Americas, but the first and second generations of Christian Americans took the gospel message deep into the wilderness of a heathen continent.

15

In Adams' Fall, We Sinned All

The first schools in America were in the home. These early schools were a result of the Puritan adherence to Scripture. Genesis 18:19 states, "He will command his children and his household after him, and they shall keep the way of the Lord."

> Family education stressed moral principles, practical skills, and family ties. Spiritual training and basic educational skills were closely associated in most colonial families. Basic skills were to be tools to gain spiritual knowledge. Thus the Bible was often used to teach children reading and reasoning as well as to impart spiritual truth.[1]

The Puritan movement for education was not to provide the child with a better job. There were no better jobs in the new continent. The motive was to deliver the child from heathenism through the reading and application of God's Word. In 1642, the Massachusetts Bay Colony passed a law requiring home education through parents or tutors, in an effort to ensure each child could read and write.

> The Massachusetts Bay Colony School Law of May 1642 is one of the earliest laws on education in the American colonies. It reflected the concern of the New England settlers, even at that early date, with establishing a uniform code of education and confirmed an awareness that family responsibility for education had been, for the most part, a failure. In the Southern colonies, on the other hand, there was less concern with a public system of education; geographic, social, and economic conditions resulted in a system of apprenticeship and vocational training for the poor, while the children of wealthy families were educated by private tutors. Both the Massachusetts act and Virginia act of 1646 ... did share, however, a common apprehension that lack of education might allow children to fall into corrupt ways.[2]

Although the Virginia law did not stipulate spiritual reasons for enacting the law, it did recognize God as blessing the colony with children.

In 1647 the Massachusetts General Court passed the Old Deluder Satan Act stating, "It being one chief project of the old deluder, Satan, to keep men from the knowledge of the Scriptures."[3] The act required that communities of 50 families appoint and pay for a teacher, and that communities of 100 families were to erect a school building and pay for basic education. The express purpose of this formal education was to teach children to read the Bible at the public's expense for the public good. It is of special note that America's first compulsory school law was enacted to teach children to read the Bible.

> During its first two hundred years, education in America was thoroughly Christian. The Bible was the chief textbook, and the children learned it well. By the turn of the 19th century, John Adams could state 'that finding an illiterate man in New England was as rare as a comet.'[4]

The curriculum for the colonial student consisted of The Bible, *The Hornbook, The New England Primer,* and *The Bay Psalm Book. The Hornbook* was basically a small hand held flash card that contained the alphabet, the Lord's Prayer and possibly a short doctrinal catechism. *The Bay Psalm Book* was the approved hymnal of the Puritans. *The New England Primer* included the listing of the books of the Bible, the Lord's Prayer, the Decalogue, the Apostle's Creed, the Westminster Shorter Catechism, and an Alphabet of Lessons for Youth. The alphabet not only taught the basic structure and phonetic sounds of the language, but also helped the students learn doctrinal and life lessons.

> A
> In ADAM'S Fall
> We sinned all.
> B
> Heaven to find;
> The Bible Mind.
> C
> Christ crucify'd
> For sinners dy'd.

The first letter of the alphabet reminded the young student of his fallen sinful nature and pointed him to his need for salvation. Truly, the New England concept of education was one that would ward off the encroachment of Satan into society, by capturing the minds of their youth for Christ. Therefore, schools were essential and the curriculum was Christian.

Higher education also had a motive much greater than that of vocation. It was ministry. The Virginia colony chartered the first college in America in 1619 at Henrico, Virginia. Henricus College was founded on the principles of Christian faith "for the training and bringing up of infidel's children to the true knowledge of God and the understanding of righteousness."[6]

Only six years after the Puritans reached American soil, they founded Harvard College in Cambridge, Massachusetts. The institution was named for Reverend John Harvard, a Puritan minister who died shortly after coming to New England. His will directed that one-half of his estate and his entire library of over 400 books go to the college. This excerpt from *The New England First Fruits* of 1643 describes the idea of the founding of Harvard.

> After God had carried us safe to New England, and we had built our houses, provided necessaries for our livelihood, reared convenient places for God's worship, and settled the civil government, one of the next things we longed for and looked after was to advance learning and perpetuate it to posterity; dreading to leave an illiterate ministry to the churches, when our present ministers shall lie in the dust.[7]

It is estimated that over 50 percent of the seventeenth century graduates of Harvard became ministers, and countless others went on to be Christian gentlemen and civic leaders. New England was a success, basically because of the Christian influences of education, which began with the Hornbook and the Primer and completed with college textbooks, but ever wrapped around the Holy Bible continuity. Cotton Mather, the Puritan historian and Harvard alumnus said of his alma mater:

> "[T]he Christians in the most early times of New-England were to form a colledge, wherein a succession of a learned and able ministry might be educated. And, indeed, they foresaw that without such a provision for a *sufficient ministry,* the churches of New-England must have been less than a *business of one age*, and soon have come to

nothing; the other *hemisphere* of the world would never have sent us over men enough to have answered our necessities; but without a nursery for such men among ourselves 'darkness must have covered the land, and gross darkness the people.'"[8]

Harvard's "Rules and Precepts," adopted in 1646, testify to the strong Christian foundation of the institution.

Let every student be plainly instructed, and earnestly pressed to consider well, the main end of his life and studies is, to know God and Jesus Christ which is eternal life (John 17:3) and therefore lay Christ at the bottom, as the only foundation of all sound knowledge and learning. And seeing the Lord only giveth wisdom, Let every one seriously set himself by prayer in secret to seek it of him, Proverbs 2:3.

Every one shall so exercise himself in reading the Scriptures twice a day, that he shall be ready to give such an account of his proficiency therein, both in *Theoretical* observations of the language, and *Logic*, and in *Practical* and spiritual truths, as his Tutor shall require, according to his ability; seeing *the entrance of the word giveth light, it giveth understanding to the simple*, Psalm 119:130.[9]

By the dawning of the eighteenth century, many New Englanders believed that Harvard had drifted from its fundamental moorings. In an effort to stem the tide of theological liberalism, Yale College was founded at New Haven, Connecticut in 1701.

Yale in the early 1700s stated as its primary goal that 'every student shall consider the main end of his study to wit to know God in Jesus Christ and answerably to lead a Godly, sober life.'[10]

William and Mary College was chartered in 1662, but not opened until 1693 at Williamsburg, Virginia. It was founded as an Anglican college to glorify and honor Jesus Christ and further Christianity in the colony. The Statutes of the College state its reason for existence.

There are three things which the Founders of this College proposed to themselves, to which all its Statutes should be directed.

The first is that the youth of Virginia should be well educated to learning and good morals.

The second is that the churches of America, especially Virginia, should be supplied with good ministers after the doctrine and government of the Church of England, and that the college should be a constant seminary for this purpose.

The Third is that the Indians of America should be instructed in the Christian religion, and that some of the Indian youth that are well behaved and well inclined, being first well prepared in the Divinity School, may be sent out to preach the gospel to their countrymen in their own tongue, after they have duly been put in orders of deacons and priests.[11]

Columbia University of New York City was founded in 1754 under the name of Kings College. The college's statement of purpose was, "The chief thing that is aimed at in this college is to teach and engage children to know God in Jesus Christ."[12]

Princeton was founded in 1746 by New Jersey Presbyterians, who sought to train ministers to make an impact on the middle colonies. The results of Princeton went further than its founder dreamed. One of its early presidents, John Witherspoon, is said to be "the man who shaped the men of America."

Most of the colleges founded during the colonial period had Christian origins, as the following chart illustrates.

The Growth of Colonial Higher Education			
College	Year	Founders	Location
Harvard	1636	Puritans	Cambridge, Massachusetts
William & Mary	1693	Anglicans	Williamsburg, Virginia
Yale	1701	Puritans	New Haven, Connecticut
College of Philadelphia	1740	Nonsectarian	Philadelphia, Pennsylvania
Princeton	1746	Presbyterians	Princeton, New Jersey
Columbia	1754	Episcopalians	New York, New York
Brown	1764	Baptists	Providence, Rhode Island
Rutgers	1766	Dutch Reformed	New Brunswick, New Jersey
Dartmouth	1769	Puritans	Hanover, New Hampshire

The philosophy of education in New England was diametrically opposed to that of the Old World. In Europe especially, a college education was limited to the social elite. The lower classes were deemed unfit to be formally educated. In contrast, the New England Puritans viewed literacy not as refinement, but as enlightenment to the inner man to follow the leadership of Christ. The regenerated man would then mold his entire being around his relationship to God through the Scriptures. To be unable to read the Scriptures would render one unable to properly function in life. Therefore, education, to the New Englander, was not a dear luxury but a dire necessity.

16

Wars and Rumors of War

God had divinely placed the Pilgrims in the wilderness of Massachusetts following the epidemic that decimated the Patuxet Indians in 1619. Then, through the miraculous turn of events with Samoset, Squanto and Massasoit, the Pilgrims had negotiated a treaty of peace with the Wampanoag tribe in 1620. But, upon the death of Chief Massasoit, the peaceful Wampanoags began to be weary of the English ways. The English Pilgrims and Puritans who sought the Indian land usually traded or made treaties for it, but often the Indians felt that they were cheated by the English. Another point of contention was the Indians who had been converted to Christianity.

Through the efforts of missionaries like John Elliot and the Mayhews, thousands of Indians had come to Christ. Along with Christianity, many had followed the European way of life. They left their tribal villages and moved to English-style settlements. These "Praying Indians" were rejecting the cultures of their ancestors and their families. In 1675,

Metacomet, the son of Massasoit and leader of the Wampanoags, began talking to other chiefs about attacking the settlers. His motive was to rid the country of Christians. Though these rumors were common, no such uprising had materialized. John Sassamon, a converted Indian, exposed this plot to Governor John Winslow. Sassamon was then murdered by three other Indians. An eye-witness testified at the trial of the three murderers. They were tried by two courts to ensure the utmost of civil fairness. One jury was composed of settlers and the other of the wisest Indians (Pilgrim point of view) in the colony. Both juries rendered the same guilty verdict unanimously. The three Indians were hung for their crime, but as fate would have it, a rope broke on one of the convicted Indians. One murderer fell to the ground, and in an instant confessed to the crime. He was hung a second time, and Plymouth learned the truth of their Christian brother's death. Upon learning of the three Indians' execution at the hands of the Pilgrims, Chief Metacomet (the settlers gave him the Christian name Philip) swore vengeance upon the Christians. Indian bands sent out raiding parties against the settlers. Men, women and children alike were brutally terrorized and killed. Small settlements were laid waste. The Pilgrims would have been totally exterminated if it had not been for the aid of the "Praying Indians."

By the summer of 1676, the settlers began to be hunters instead of the hunted. They would pursue the savages into the woods and hunt them on their own terrain. Upon leaving to search for raiding parties, the settlers would call upon their friends to "pray for us and we will fight for you."[1] The terror lasted for weeks as Indians raided English towns, and the settlers countered by killing Indians.

However, there were some positive results of King Philip's War.

> So many people had sincerely and publicly repented of their sinful ways, so many lives were truly reformed, so many broken relationships were restored, and so many churches solemnly renewed their covenants that God relented and poured out His mercy. There was a sense of freshness in the colonies, a sense of cleanness, and new hope. The colonies were united in a common cause, while Satan's house again divided against itself, along the lines of the ancient tribal rivalries. Now 'luck' seemed to be running so much against the Indians that they began giving themselves up, in small bands, and then in droves.[2]

In August of 1676, Philip was killed by an ambush and the Wampanoags surrendered. King Philip's War was over.

> Relative to the region's population, the war was the costliest in American history. On a proportionate basis, it took more lives and destroyed more property than any other. The English lost more than six hundred fighting men and uncounted civilians. Nearly half of their towns were torched and abandoned;

twelve hundred houses and thousands of bushels of grain were burned; eight thousand head of cattle were killed. Even so, the Indians suffered worse. Perhaps nine thousand of Philip's twelve thousand supporters and allies died from wounds, exposure or starvation; another two thousand fled the region."[3]

Both societies were devastated, but both survived. The Wampanoags were later absorbed into other Indian tribes. The Pilgrims, as well, became a small part of a greater picture in the history of New England, but both were permanently woven in the fabric that we now call America.

At the same time King Philip's War was raging in Massachusetts, a settler's rebellion broke out in Virginia. The dispute was over Governor William Berkeley's inability to protect English settlers from Indian attack. The Virginia settlers had not been as careful in their dealings with the Indians as the New Englanders. By 1675, the settlers had pushed out of the Tidewater region, and the natives resented the "white man's" intrusion in their lands. One summer day in 1675, an Indian was discovered killing a settler in his own house. The English colonists were immediately terrified at the thought of a wholesale Indian uprising. Settlers began to take law and revenge into their own hands. Governor Berkeley dispatched troops to defend the colonists, but a dispute ensued when he disbanded a volunteer army of 300 Virginians. From this group of rebels, led by Nathaniel Bacon, 60 formed armed resistance against the governor's troops and continued to harass the Indians. For months, tyranny and terror reigned in Virginia. Finally, Governor Berkeley regained control of the militia, and Bacon's Rebellion ceased when Bacon mysteriously died. Peace once again came to the Virginia frontier, and the rebellion of 1676 died with its instigator.

17

Pilgrim's Progress

What began as a tiny trickle of European immigrants to the New World in 1620, developed into a massive flood by the last days of the century. The beleaguered English Christians who populated Plymouth became known by the Biblical name of Pilgrims, probably coined by their Governor William Bradford. Bradford's perspective of their venture was much like that of Abraham's, recorded in Hebrews 11:8-16. The Pilgrims departed "not knowing whither he (they) went ... in a strange country ... and confessed that they were strangers and pilgrims on earth." The analogy fit and the terminology stuck. The Pilgrims were religious pioneers in a "strange country."

Their Puritan brethren followed and quickly surrounded them in Massachusetts. The Puritans carried the analogy of Abraham further than the Pilgrims. The Puritans accepted their relationship with God as a covenant, just as the Abrahamic Covenant directed the father of the Hebrews to a new land, so God would covenantly provide for His children, the Puritans. This idea was helped by political events in England. In 1629, King Charles I cleaned out the "nest of vipers" by dissolving Parliament and jailing Puritan leaders. Since Charles did not reconvene Parliament for 11 years, this left the Puritans without a voice in religious or civil affairs. Since the survival of reformed Protestantism seemed doomed in England, the Puritans began to look at New England as their true promised land, and migrated in masses. Religious persecution continued in England for two long decades. On January 30, 1649, Charles I was beheaded for crimes against the English people. A Commonwealth was established with the victorious General Oliver Cromwell as the Lord Protector and chief executive of the land. One might have thought that the immigration to the New World would have slowed once the unbearable religious persecution of the Mother Country stopped. This simply was not what happened for several reasons. First of all, immediately after the execution of Charles I, the Virginia colony declared its loyalty to the English royal house of Stuart and offered safe haven to fleeing English cavaliers. Since the cavaliers supported Charles, multitudes came to Virginia to resume their lives in exile.

Secondly, since the days of Henry VIII, England had constantly been torn by religious unrest. The party in power not only controlled civil but also religious life. Though Oliver Cromwell was a staunch Puritan, he was never willing to seize power in England. This made the permanent protection of New England safer than the temporary protection of the Lord Protector.

The third reason was that to the seventeenth century English Protestant, there was always a threat of Great Britain reverting to the bonds of Catholicism. This threat was very much alive as long as Charles's son by the same name, and heir to the throne, was in exile in the Catholic stronghold of France. Early in Cromwell's administration, Charles II raised a formidable army financed by the French monarch and invaded England to claim the throne for the House of Stuart. Charles was defeated in 1651 and returned to exile in France, but he would ascend to the British throne nine years later at the request of the English people, once again attempting to re-establish Catholicism as the religion of England.

Another reason the immigration to the New World did not stop was that the religious liberties of the English colonies in America were extremely inviting to deeply religious Englishmen. To the Puritan, New England was a spiritual haven. Disgruntled Anglicans could enjoy the structure of the Anglican Church in colonial Virginia as well as the distance from the Mother Church in London. Maryland, Pennsylvania, New York and Rhode Island supplied even more religious toleration, even for the Catholics. As a whole, the colonies were a paradise for those seeking religious freedom.

Another prime motivation for immigration was not only the freedom of religion, but also the freedom to succeed. America was growing at a phenomenal rate. "There were approximately 5,000 settlers living in America in 1630; 50,368 in 1650; 250,888 in 1700, 629,000 in 1730, and 1,170,760 in 1750."[1] The growth rate in the colonies is indicative of the success of the colonial experiment prompted by the volatile religious climate of Europe in the seventeenth to eighteenth centuries.

> The first actual census of the population in America was made in 1790. A much later scholarly analysis of that census concluded that the white population was composed of the following national stocks: 'English 60.9, Scotch 8.3, Ulster Irish [probably mostly Scotch-Irish] 6, Free State Irish 3.7, German 8.7, Dutch 3.4, French 1.7, unassigned 6.6.'[2]

When Puritanism briefly ruled under Oliver Cromwell in the mid 1600s, England was not without her problems. In 1653, Cromwell dissolved Parliament, proclaiming it "a conclave of corrupt and unjust men ... scandalous to the profession of the Gospel."[3] In its place, he gathered a group of men called the Assembly of Saints, which he hoped would govern in the "fear of God." Cromwell gave the following instruction:

> "Be pitiful ... and tender towards all though of different judgments ... Love all, tender all, cherish and countenance all, in all things that are good ... And if the poorest Christian, the most mistaken Christian, shall desire to live peaceably and quietly under you – I say, if

any shall desire but to lead a life of godliness and honesty, let him be protected."[4]

Apparently, the Puritan Cromwell failed to recognize the Puritan doctrine of depravity in his Parliament, even though he recognized the sovereignty of God as he ruled through his executive. The Lord Protector stated, "It matters not who is our Commander in Chief if God be so."[5] Cromwell never aspired to seize the reins of government, nor did he prepare for his son and successor to do so. Richard resigned only months after becoming the Lord Protector.

On May 25, 1660, Charles II was crowned King of England. The monarchy was restored to the Stuart family. The pendulum of religious authority swiftly and abruptly swung to the left as Charles ascended the throne. The leftward movement did not slow until Catholicism was once again enthroned in England. Puritans immediately lost their places in religion and society. Many were jailed and executed.

> Dissenting Protestants could be brought up on charges and fined or sent to prison. Property and business assets of the accused were frequently seized to pay fines. The prisons were overcrowded, disease-ridden, cold, and filthy beyond human tolerance. Charles seemed to have repealed Cromwell's legacy, and appeared to be pulling England's political system back into the Middle Ages.[6]

Suppressive acts to regulate the free course of religious expression were pushed through Parliament by the popish king. Puritan ministers were excommunicated and not allowed within five miles of their former parish (The Five Mile Act of 1665). Religious and civil tyranny reigned under Charles II. The outcome was that hundreds more English Protestants flocked to the colonies to avoid religious persecution. These were the days that John Bunyan languished in Bedford's jail for preaching the Gospel. These were also the dark days that propelled John Locke to the English spotlight, and a century later into the hearts of American idealists, such as Adams, Jefferson and Franklin. It was the turbulent times of English history that eventually birthed the religious and civil freedoms of America. Though it seemed to a countless many that God was nowhere to be found, He was quietly and ever so carefully moving His standard to be planted on another shore in another hemisphere.

Without a doubt, the freedom to worship God and to exercise one's religious beliefs was one of the foundational reasons for multitudes coming to America. However, that was not the only reason to settle in the New World. In fact, religion was far from the minds of many in colonial America. There was also the multitude who were neither spiritually hot nor cold. In reality, the colonists brought a mission field with them. From the beginning, each colony was a melting pot of religious beliefs. Puritanism reigned in New England, Quakerism in Penn's colony, Anglicanism in Virginia and the south, while other groups were intermixed throughout the eastern seaboard. Each area had some sort of Gospel witness very early in its founding. Each colony was also somewhat intolerant of other religious groups. Rhode Island and Maryland, by nature of their founding, were basically free and open to most religious groups. The Quakers were more tolerant than the Puritans to other "religious brothers," but in the southern colonies, the ones who did not have a bedrock foundation of religious beliefs, the intolerance was sharp. Chambers and Fisher explain the role of Anglicanism in America;

> Although some early settlers at Jamestown were Puritans, the leaders were mostly Anglicans. The Anglican church, theologically midway between Puritanism and Catholicism, tended to shift its views toward first one and then the other. During the late seventeenth century, the church had shifted toward Catholicism's formalism, but it still preserved the Thirty-Nine Articles, which had a strong biblical and evangelical emphasis.
>
> There were differing views within the Anglican church as well. Those who supported formalism and ritual were called High Church Anglicans; those who favored strong biblical preaching and were less interested in ritual were known as Low Church Anglicans. Most of the Anglican settlers at Jamestown were Low Church.[7]

Though Baptists were present in the early days of the Massachusetts colony, they began an exodus in haste from England during the persecution under the pro-Catholic monarchs, Charles II and James II. These protestors were of a different stripe. Historian Don Boys says this of his Baptist ancestors:

> "We did not come out of the Reformation – we were **before** the Reformation. We never did come out of the Roman Catholic Church because we never went into it.
>
> "Sir Isaac Newton said that it was his conviction that '*the Baptists were the only Christians who had not symbolized with Rome.*' No, Baptists were not new-comers on the religious scene. Even Luther (who had no love for Baptists) said, '*The Anabaptists have been for a long time spreading in Germany.*'
>
> "Two writers (members of the Reformed Church) investigated the claim of Baptists that they were of an early origin and wrote: '*On this account the Baptists may be considered as the only Christian community which has stood since the days of the apostles and as a Christian society which has preserved the doctrines of the Gospel through all ages.*'"[8]

In the closing days of the seventeenth century, Baptist dissenters began to make their way to Virginia and the Carolinas in large numbers. Though most

Anglican churches practiced a Low Church type of worship, the Baptists could not accept the worship, identification with the Church of England, or some of their foundational doctrines. Most Baptists lacked education, funding or a following. They did possess tenacity, and a love for the Scriptures. The Baptist problem was the State Church, Anglican. To preach and perform their "religion" in these colonies required a license from the state. Religious intolerance and persecution were nothing new to Baptists. Edward Hiscox writes of them in *The New Directory for Baptist Churches*.

> Many thousands of the Dutch Baptists, called Anabaptists and Mennonites, miserably perished by the hands of their cruel persecutors for no crime but their refusal to conform to established churches. At what time the Baptists appeared in England in definite denominational form, it is impossible to say. But from the *twelfth* to the *seventeenth* century, many of them suffered cruel persecutions, and death by burning, drowning, and beheading, besides many other and sometimes most inhuman tortures. And this they suffered both from Papists and Protestants, condemned by both civil and ecclesiastical tribunals, only because they persisted in worshipping God according to the dictates of their consciences, and because they would not submit their religious faith and worship to the dictates of popes and princes.[9]

Once Baptist preachers reached the "Promised Land," they continued to experience ecclesiastical persecution as they did in Europe.

> During the early years of Virginia's history, no minister was permitted to preach unless he had received ordination from an Anglican bishop across the sea. Attendance at the Episcopalian church was mandatory with absentees being fined 50 pounds of tobacco. With the ascension of William and Mary following England's Glorious Revolution, this ecclesiastical monopoly was technically dissolved by the Toleration Act of 1689. Dissenting clergy could now apply for a license provided they would ascribe to the Anglican Articles of Religion (excluding articles 34, 35, and 36, with a rewording of 20) denounce the Romish doctrines of transubstantiation and Mariolatry, affirm as abhorrent the Jesuit doctrine of political assassination and swear allegiance to their Majesties, William and Mary.[10]

The Baptist opposition was the fiercest in New England and Virginia. The first century of Baptist growth was slow. Baptist immigrants were few and scattered.

> They were still dissentients from the majority of their fellow Christians, by whom they were defamed, opposed, and persecuted. Though

in this country none were burned, hanged, or drowned because of their faith yet in New England they were banished, fined, imprisoned, and publicly whipped at the stake because they insisted on religious liberty and would not submit to the magistrates in matters of faith and conscience.[11]

Since Baptist fervor for repentance and evangelism was greater than most denominations of the late seventeenth and early eighteenth century, they encountered opposition from the world as well as the worldly church. From the rural Virginia mission field, one account reads like this:

With multitudes of the resultant converters deserting their dead Episcopalian churches, the inevitable backlash of historic persecution brought about the most ignominious chapter in Old Dominion history. Throughout this period, Satan tested both the preachers' resolve and the people's reaction by initiating his opposition through an unrestrained rabble of the baser sort. While a preacher's sermon could be interrupted by the unexpected arrival of a snake or hornet's nest being tossed in through an open window, or the outright smashing to bits of his pulpit and communion table, his baptismal candidates might be scattered in the local creek by a mob of mounted drunks. When one gang violently submerged Reverend David Barrow and a fellow pastor seven times, and then asked him if they 'believed,' the exasperated but colorful preacher replied, 'I believe you mean to drown me.'[12]

The Baptist churches of America progressed slowly. They had no mass exodus like the Puritans. They did not colonize a region like the Pilgrims, but they did meet intense opposition like no other groups in America. They were opposed by other religious groups, by the world and by Baptists themselves. Even though there is no documented decline in the Baptist fervor or fidelity in the first half of the eighteenth century, as was found in most other religious groups, they fell prey to themselves. Calvinistic and Armenian groups constantly looted each other's camp. By the close of the eighteenth century, northern Calvinistic Baptists were sending missionaries to the South to evangelize the General Baptists of North Carolina.

18

A Sleeping Giant

How could the "New Israel" forget God? With a century of advancement, religiously, civilly, and economically, God had blessed them in every way. How could these Pilgrims and Strangers forget the God who had so graciously given them the Promised Land? It was simple – just like the "Old Israel" did. They were caught up in the blessings of the Promised Land and forgot the source of their blessings. They forgot their Maker, and their mission. By the turn of the eighteenth century, America was in a spiritual and moral decline. Salem had survived the witch trials (there were trials in other colonies as well), Plymouth was crippled by King Philip's War, and the southern colonies were struggling with Anglicanism. Many settlements had an increase in crime, vice and lawlessness. Drunkenness, robbery, counterfeiting, and gambling were common in most towns.

Immorality became more common as time went on. William Penn described

Philadelphia in these words: 'There is no place more overrun with wickedness. Sins so very Scandalous, openly Committed in defiance of Law and Virtue: the facts so foul, I am forbid by Common modesty to relate.' One man in Boston wrote of the 'Levity and Wanton Frollicks of the Young People, who, when their Devotion's over, have recourse to the Ordinaries [taverns], where they plentifully wash away the remembrance of their Old Sins, and drink down the fear of a Fine, or the dread of a Whipping-post.' One Parson Phillips, an Anglican minister in Philadelphia, spoke freely of his immorality; he was called 'a most vile man, not only in practice but in conversation, and he still holds the church and a number of hearers.'[1]

The results of this human depravity were throughout the colonies. No colony was exempt and no profession was beyond the touch of man's fallen nature.

There were several factors that contributed to the decline of religion in colonial life. One reason was that of unfaithful pastors. Many pastors came to America for a new start. Instead, they brought their old problems with them. Others were following a vocation rather than a vision. A great number of religious leaders may have been spiritually unqualified. Although well educated, many were apparently unconverted. Some merely lost their zeal for the work in a hard new land. As the second and third generations of Puritans failed to pass the torch of their beliefs to the next generation, so their pastors failed in the same way. Churches became tolerant of sins because pastors ceased to preach of specific sins. As a result, communities practiced more sin. In time, even the basic doctrines began to be forsaken. The Separatist Puritans failed to be separated or even preach the doctrine of separation that was so dear to them. The New England Purists also began to lose their vision for the covenant with God and their mission to reach the lost.

A second reason for the religious decline was that more and more church members were unconverted and therefore uninterested. They would rather die than not be a Puritan, but many had never converted to the Puritan doctrine of salvation by grace, evidenced by change in one's life. The Puritan erroneous belief in infant baptism was the bedrock of their error. By baptizing infants, parents and child alike were given a false hope and distorted view of salvation. Their strict adherence to ecclesiastical and civil laws required one to be active in religion but often allowed one to neglect the true relationship with God through Jesus Christ. These unregenerate churchmen posed a problem for the church. William Grady describes the outcome:

> On June 4, 1657, a historic gathering of Puritan ministers assembled in Boston for a meeting that would signal the beginning of the end for their New England theocracy. The issue under discussion involved a number of

second-generation parents who wanted their own children 'baptized' (sprinkled) despite the fact that they themselves had yet to be judged regenerate by the official minister of religion. In a drastic move to allow for the superstitious christenings, the decision was made to accept the unconverted parents into the church membership with the stipulation that they refrain from communion. Known as the *Halfway Covenant*, it provided 'that all persons of sober life and correct sentiments, without being examined as to a change of heart, might profess religion or become members of the Church, and have their children baptized, though they did not come to the Lord's table.'[2]

Man's way over God's plan never works. In just a matter of years, the Puritan compromise proved to be more deadly than an Indian attack or a dreaded plague. By the early eighteenth century, most of the Puritan's Congregational churches had become ineffective as witnesses, and many of the church members had become hypocritical, priding themselves in their conformity to Puritan rules rather than loving the Lord and His Word. They had failed primarily not because non-Christians had invaded their churches, but because they had not won their own children to a personal acceptance of the gospel. But how could this happen? Were the Puritans so opposed to change that they could not modify one belief to save the entire movement? Of course the Puritans were flexible. They were people of change. Their name itself cries out for change – to come back to the purity of Scripture. They changed their homeland when they moved to a different continent. They changed civil governments. They modified their lifestyles from fine English homes to humble American huts. They gave up practically everything that they knew and loved for their relationship with God. How could they forfeit their God? They were morally afflicted from birth by their mother, the Mother Church, and the erroneous doctrine of infant baptism. The flexible Puritans that moved across the globe would not move on this one practice. Instead, they modified their covenant with God. The results were disastrous. Pastors complained of disinterested parishioners who failed in family Bible study, church attendance and consistent living. By the early eighteenth century, an interest in material goods was replacing an interest in spiritual things. The economy prospered and the prosperous lost their dependence upon God.

A third reason for religious decline was unqualified educators. Spiritual deadness in America at this time can be traced in part to a spiritual decline in the institutions of higher education. Many church leaders were still being trained in liberal British institutions, but America's few colleges were in decline too. Since colleges tend to exalt knowledge and reason over faith, they often experience spiritual decline before other institutions. Note the sad state of affairs at America's "flagship" university, Harvard:

By the eighteenth century, a growing number of New England colonists believed that Harvard had drifted from its original course. Increase Mather, president of Harvard from 1685 to 1701, and his son Cotton Mather, had hoped they could prevent Harvard from moving away from its original Calvinistic orientation. They failed. Harvard not only moved beyond Calvinism to Armenianism, but drifted on to Unitarianism.[3]

It was only a matter of time until Yale fell into darkness also, and the same legacy continues today when unchecked higher education stresses reason over responsibility, and knowledge over knowing the King of Kings.

Unstable situations also led to a weakening of Christianity. America was still an infant country in 1700. In fact, she was no more than a land of separate, distinctly different colonies, none more than a century old. And yet she, America, as a whole had survived. Massachusetts survived the heretical halfway covenant; Salem overcame the hysteria of the witches; Philadelphia endured the deadly plague; and rural Virginia continued after Bacon's treacherous rebellion. Infant America was still alive, but not well. These trials had taken a toll on the American spirit. Through each trial, she had come, but was weakened by the tribulation. The occult influence manifested at Salem, the spiritual deadness of Anglicanism, and the spiritual waywardness of Puritanism all pointed to the sickness of the land. Williams' experiment in

Rhode Island and Baltimore's settlement in Maryland had become not only tolerant of religion, but of sin as well. The European Rationalism was beginning to raise its ugly head in America. Scientific advancements had caused some to place more confidence in science than in God. As the seventeenth century came to a close and the eighteenth dawned, it seemed America was doomed to follow in the same path as her European ancestors. But God had other plans for America, His New Israel. Her hope was in her reaction to God's chastisement – repent and live.

19

The Great Awakening

While America slept in her sin and complacency, God was shaking her in an attempt to rouse her from her sin and rebellion. For over a century, the colonies had drawn from the bountiful supply of the Almighty. She had basked in His mercy and grace and thrived on His providential care. The sky was the limit for the booming British colonies. But, they were not looking to the skies for spiritual direction, neither were they gazing upon the Old Country for financial aid. America was becoming self-sufficient, in need of no one or any foreign land, and God alone could see that stubborn arrogance wrapped around the American pioneering spirit. That humble spirit that propelled them to conquer the savage wilderness, as they trusted in God to sustain them, was now being supplanted by the same selfish lust for more that cost Adam his paradise. The seventeenth century had dawned with no Englishmen on American soil. By century's end, the entire eastern seaboard was dotted with successful British colonies.

God had sustained them, but by the third generation, America was losing touch with God. It was man who had become lost, but it would be God who sent out a search party to find His lost people. The search party was an army of God-sent messengers, preachers, pastors and revivalists. Many of these people, the world will never remember, while a handful still live today in the annals of American history.

As with most revivals, it is difficult to determine when the Great Awakening began. The origin, of course, is God. The object is man. But when did the Great Awakening begin? In *The Light and the Glory,* Marshall and Manuel propose a date.

> In 1734, the lightning began to strike America. And indeed, nothing short of a series of lightning bolts could have awakened this slumbering Christian giant who had eaten so much prosperity pudding, washed down with goblet after goblet of the wine of self-satisfaction. As the place for the first bolt to fall, God chose Northampton, Massachusetts, the little town of the most learned and respected theologian which America had yet produced. Jonathan Edwards was a brilliant, but reserved and dry, Puritan preacher, who delivered his sermons in a monotone, with his eyes never straying from the back wall of the church.[1]

Though Jonathan Edwards was definitely a key player in the revival that probably saved America, he may not have been the original kindling that set the colonies ablaze for righteousness. The pietistic Dutch evangelist Theodore Jacob Frelinghuysen may have been the original spark.

> Because of these critical influences upon other Presbyterian and Reformed clergymen, Frelinghuysen deserves to be remembered as an important herald, if not the father, of the Great Awakening. Whatever the size of his awakening, his contributions to the restructuring of a ministry concerned with and organized for revival, and to the disciplining of the churches involved, assure Frelinghuysen a place among those inculcating this ecclesiology in the American church.[2]

The Tennants of New Jersey, or the powerful evangelist George Whitefield, are also looked to as founders of the Great Awakening. From God's perspective, it may have been some long-forgotten praying mother or saintly father. Nevertheless, the revival was astounding.

> The evangelical movement took the emphasis away from the doctrine, from forms and ritual, and from what, in more general terms, may be called 'churchiness.' What was essential was not outward conformity to religious forms but inward conversion, a new heart, and a new man. To such an outlook, an established church tended to be only so much dead weight. The revival movement stressed

individual conversion and piety, and the improvement of society by way of improved men and women. The way to community was not through government power but by changed people. Thus, the Great Awakening cut across the bounds of colonies and denominations to provide a common ground in evangelical religion to many inhabitants throughout the colonies.[3]

Revival began to break out in villages and towns across the middle and northern colonies. In the woods of rural Pennsylvania, Theodore Frelinghuysen's preaching began to take hold. Sinners would cry out for forgiveness as the spiritual groundswell began to build. Frelinghuysen was not without opposition. His doctrine and practices were continually called to question by jealous "ministers of the Gospel" who stated he was unorthodox in his belief of personal conversion, in the administration of communion and in his criticism of other clergy. Nevertheless, Frelinghuysen's work continued as a work of evangelism in the middle colonies. Gilbert and William Tennant joined the Dutch evangelist in the 1720s, thereby uniting Dutch Reformed and Presbyterians for the common good, revival. This tie made evangelism the chief goal. They traveled the hills and hamlets of Pennsylvania, New Jersey, New York and Delaware, quietly ushering thousands into the kingdom of God.

Jonathan Edwards, America's greatest theologian, was pastor of the Northampton Congregational

Church in Northampton, Massachusetts when his ministry was incorporated into the Great Awakening. He speaks of revival in a 1734 entry in his journal.

> 'The Spirit of God began extraordinarily to set in, and wonderfully to work among us; and there were very suddenly, one after another, five or six persons who were to all appearances savingly converted, and some of them wrought upon in a very remarkable manner.' His *Faithful Narrative of the Surprising Work of God* was an attempt to objectively report what happened, and Edwards attributed all to the work of the Almighty among the townspeople; 'This work of God, as it was carried on, and the number of true saints multiplied, soon made a glorious alteration in the town; so that in the spring and summer following anno 1735, the town seemed to be full of the presence of God; it was never so full of love, nor of joy, and yet so full of distress, as it was then. There were remarkable tokens of God's presence in almost every house. It was a time of joy in families on account of salvation being brought unto them.'[4]

In one year, God had blessed Edwards' work more than the 60-year ministry of Solomon Stoddard, the grandfather and predecessor at the Northampton Church. Edwards went on to conduct revival meetings in the area – all with great success. His messages were well prepared, but delivered in a monotone voice. He hardly ever looked at his audience. The power was in the Holy Spirit's movement and the preached Word of God. Through the entire season of refreshing and harvest of souls, Edwards retained a humble spirit.

> Such cool and studied detachment was typical of Edwards' attitude. He refused to identify himself as chief source or exponent of revivalistic activities, not so much out of modesty as out of his belief that people are mere means for God's designs. Edwards desired to disclaim leadership of the awakening and took few active measures to further it himself.[5]

In November of 1739, the famed British evangelist, George Whitefield arrived in Philadelphia. He was immediately enlisted by the Tennants to aid in the "New Light" cause in the middle colonies. The "New Lights," as they were called, were Presbyterians or Congregationalists who espoused the new movement as a true revival of God. Immediately thousands came to Christ at the preaching of Whitefield. He preached non-stop in Pennsylvania, New Jersey, the Carolinas and finally in Georgia, where he established a home for orphans. In September of 1740, Whitefield sailed for the Citadal of Puritanism – New England. In Boston, the News-Letter reported on his success.

> "He preached in the forenoon at the South Church to a crowded audience, and in the

afternoon to about 5,000 people on the Common; and Lord's Day in the afternoon, having preached to a great number of people at the Old Brick Church, the house not being large enough to hold those that crowded to hear him. When the exercise was over, he went and preached in the field, to at least 8,000 persons."[6]

But not all appreciated Whitefield. He often put the blame for cold, dead churches at the feet of dead preachers. On a Boston street one day, the Episcopalian Joseph Culter accosted him by smartly saying, "I am sorry to see you here." Undaunted, the famous revivalist replied, "So is the devil."[7] For over a month, his crowds continued to increase. On Sunday, October 12, his farewell sermon was heard by an estimated 30,000 Bostonians. Upon departing Boston, he examined and noted the "low spiritual tone" at Harvard, then made his way to Northampton to "compare methods" with Jonathan Edwards. Whitefield preached to thousands regularly in open air meetings, or "field preaching," which reminded him of the ministry of Jesus.

'When churches were open to him, he preached as a priest of the Church of England; when churches were closed he preached in the field. Always he had great effect.' Lord Bolingbroke referred to Whitefield as 'The most extraordinary man in our times. He has the most commanding eloquence I ever heard in any person: his abilities are very considerable; his zeal unquenchable; his piety and excellence genuine – unquestionable.'[8]

For three decades, Whitefield preached up and down the eastern seaboard. He made 13 trans-Atlantic crossings and preached an estimated 18,000 times to 60 million hearers. In the fall of 1770, the weak and exhausted revivalist was in Exeter, New Hampshire, where a crowd amassed and called for him to preach. Whitefield prayed, "Lord Jesus, I am weary in Thy work but not of it. If I have not finished my course let me go and speak for Thee once more in the fields, and seal Thy truth and come home and die." The aging evangelist could hardly preach above a whisper. He stood in humble silence for several minutes then said, "I will wait for the gracious assistance of God. For he will, I am certain, assist me once more to speak in His name."[9] He preached for nearly two hours, The next morning he was dead. The great evangelist was gone, but the effects of the Great Awakening still linger to this day.

From a time of spiritual deadness to revival speaks of a profound change. What is the legacy of the Great Awakening? First of all, tens of thousands of people were saved. Lives and families were changed forever. America was still tender and made the right choice between revival or ruin.

Secondly, hundreds of churches were established. The Congregationalists, Dutch Reformed, and Presbyterians all benefited greatly from the Awakening. William Grady stated that the Baptists may have benefited the most, not through revival of deadness, but due to their stand on separation.

An even more important result of the Awakening was the swift and wide extension of Baptist principles and churches. This was altogether logical. The revival had come, not so much in the spirit and power of Elijah, turning to each other the hearts of the fathers and of children, as in the spirit of Ezekiel, the preacher of individual responsibility and duty. The temper of the revival was wholly congenial with the strong individualism of the Baptist churches. The Separatist churches formed in New England by the withdrawal of revival enthusiasts from the parish churches in many instances became Baptist. Cases of individual conversion to Baptist views were frequent, and the earnestness with which the new opinion was held approved itself not only by debating and proselytizing, but by strenuous and useful evangelizing. Especially in the south, from Virginia to Georgia, the new preachers, entering into the labors of the annoyed and persecuted pioneers of the communion, won multitudes of converts to the Christian faith, from the neglected populations, both black and white, and gave to the Baptist churches a lasting prominence in numbers among the churches of the South.[10]

The spread of organized religion in America owes its heritage to the Great Awakening of the eighteenth century.

Thirdly, there was a phenomenal growth of colleges and universities at this time. Nearly 50 are founded as the result of George Whitefield's ministry alone. The University of Pennsylvania started as a result of an assembly hall being built by Benjamin Franklin and friends for Whitefield in Philadelphia. The institution grew from that one hall to a great university. Princeton University was also started at this time by evangelist William Tennant and became a conservative bastion for the Presbyterians for two centuries. Education fed evangelism. An example was Dartmouth College which was started to train Native American evangelists. Hundreds of young pioneering Americans were trained to carry the gospel to the frontier of America. The revival of missionary emphasis was a result of the Awakening. Although David Brainerd was a spark that helped ignite the spiritual fires of revival, when his short life ended, missionary endeavors were ablaze for years. The Great Awakening caused men to look westward and to move into the wilderness. This may have been America's first thought of manifest destiny, not only reaching the Pacific, but reaching it for God. This was a renewal of the Puritan Covenant and Americans carried it beyond the Alleghenies.

The Great Awakening woke Americans up to the reality of personal as well as religious liberty. The long decline in colonial faith subsided with the powerful preaching and sincere repentance of the Great Awakening. This revival is a particularly wonderful example of the Holy Spirit's use of a few yielded and faithful men and women who were willing to sacrifice for the good of the country.

Puritan vision and theology were both revived by the Great Awakening. Nearly strangled by the halfway covenant, then nearly consumed by modernism, the old doctrines of John Calvin were embraced once again in colonial America during the Awakening.

> The famous German historian, Ranke, one of the profound scholars of modern times says ... 'John Calvin was the virtual founder of America,' ... These revolutionary principles of republican liberty and self-government, taught and embodied in the system of Calvin, were brought to America, and in this new land where they have borne so mighty a harvest, were planted by whose hands? – the hands of the Calvinists. The vital relation of Calvin and Calvinism to the founding of the free institutions of America, however strange in some ears the statement of Ranke may have sounded, is recognized and affirmed by historians of all lands and creeds.[11]

These old foundational doctrines of the sovereignty of God and the depravity of man were preached with new fervor in the first half of the eighteenth century. Jonathan Edwards' classic sermon "Sinners in the Hands of an Angry God" is the hallmark of Calvinism and the Awakening. Not only were

Americans made aware of personal and religious liberties, but they began to focus on civil liberties as well. If the individual was to be accountable for his sin, the king must be accountable as well. This was a revival of the covenant view of government. The ruler was subordinate to the laws of God. At this time, the seeds of unconcern were sown with the Mother Country. Americans were enjoying the freedom from the bondage of Satan. It would not be long before they longed for freedom from England as well.

The Great Awakening was the colonies' first national revival. It galvanized colonists into Americans. It also provided them a higher and nobler purpose, to refocus on the intent of their founding fathers.

> "Through the almost universal, almost simultaneous experience of the Great Awakening, we began to become aware of ourselves as a *nation*, a body of believers which had a national identity as a people chosen by God for a specific purpose: to be not just 'a city upon a hill,' but a veritable citadel of Light in a darkened world. The Pilgrims had seen it, especially Bradford; so had such Puritans as Winthrop and Hooker and the Mathers. But they had all died away, and the vision of the covenant relationship had seemed to die with them. Now, through the shared experience of coming together in large groups to hear the Gospel of Jesus Christ, Americans were rediscovering God's plan to join them

together by His Spirit in the common cause of advancing His Kingdom. Furthermore, they were returning to another aspect of His plan — that they were to operate not as lone individualists, but in covenanted groups.

"Still another facet of this Great Awakening was its emphasis on action – to believe in Jesus Christ meant not merely discussing theology, but making life-changing decisions and acting upon them ... The new day would soon break across the nation. His dream had come true: America was a nation now – one nation under God."[12]

20

The War to Begin All Wars

An important harbinger of the final break between Great Britain and her American colonies was the French and Indian War. The war in itself was a misnomer. The French and Native Americans fought together to oust the British and her colonists, who for years had encroached upon French and Indian territories.

Control was the major cause of the French and Indian War. European powers, France and England, desired complete control in the North American continent. Both held extensive land claims. Both were essentially mercantilist in the middle of the eighteenth century. Mercantilism is the doctrine that developed after the decline of feudalism. It propagated the idea that economic interests of a country are of primary importance, and that these interests must be strengthened by the following actions of the government:

1. Increased foreign trade through colonial monopolies
2. Protection of domestic industries through governmental tariffs
3. Maintaining a strong gold and silver reserve
4. Maintaining a "favorable balance of trade"; that, is exports must exceed imports

The mercantilistic doctrine stated that a country's economic well-being must be protected at all costs. Colonies were viewed as sources of raw materials (timber, cotton, tobacco, etc.) These colonies would also be markets for the mother country's goods. Therefore, colonialism provided both raw materials and an outlet for finished goods. The European colonies in North America were seldom a cost to the government of the mother country. Most colonies were established by permission of the king, with private funding. Therefore, the risk to the monarch was minimal, but the gains were phenomenal. Wealth poured into the royal coffers. In fact, by the time of the American War of Independence in 1776, the question could have been posed as to who was the dependent, the fledgling colonies or Mother England, who fought incessantly to keep her wayward children. Under the mercantile system, a nation had two choices if it were to survive – to develop your own colonies through exploration and settlement, or conquer the colonies of other nations. This was the European legacy of the seventeenth and eighteenth centuries.

Mercantilism always led to war. For nearly 60 years, the Anglo-French conflict had raged. Three separate wars, King William's War, Queen Anne's War and King George's War, had begun and raged across western Europe. Each one of them spread, to a certain extent, to the New World. In 1754, the French and Indian War started in America. Two years later, it swept across the Atlantic to Europe.

By the mid-eighteenth century, the French controlled twice as much territory in America as the British did, but the French were traders and trappers, and their lands were sparsely populated. In contrast, the British had "dug in." They were building colonies along the eastern seaboard. Their population was more than 20 times that of the French. These settlers also had a vested interest in America; it was their home. To balance their lack of manpower, the French utilized the natives of the northeastern woods. These Indians introduced savage warfare and practices to the Anglo-French conflict. It is from this background of hit-and-run Indian tactical warfare that we again see God's hand of providence evident in American history. During an ill-advised raid in French territory at Fort Duquesne, General Edward Braddock instructed his men to charge headlong into an Indian attack. The Virginia militia Colonel George Washington warned the British commander against such an attack. However, the brash Braddock would not listen to Washington, and more than half his men were killed or wounded in the massacre. The Redcoats lost 977 men, while the French and Indians lost only 30. Mysteriously, all of the 86 British officers except George Washington were wounded or dead.

> Twice Washington's horse was shot out from under him, and twice he mounted a new. Four bullets tore through his clothes, but miraculously he remained unscathed. Washington moved unflinchingly through the shower of lead to collect hundreds of wounded soldiers, including Braddock, and loaded them into wagons. Fortunately for him, the Indians were too busy scalping and torturing to pursue Washington's wagons, or they could have butchered every single man in Braddock's force ... Incredibly, providentially ... Washington's body had not been touched, though his clothes had been shredded by gunfire.
>
> The expedition was a clear catastrophe for the British, but not for Washington. The veteran regulars marveled at his bravery, and his reputation spread throughout the colonies. 'I was saved,' said Washington, by 'the miraculous care of Providence that protected me beyond human expectation.' The story of his valor, loading the wounded into wagons without regard to his personal safety, became legendary.[1]

Another act of providence occurred when a French fleet with 8,000 men sailed from Canada to destroy the English settlements along the Atlantic seaboard. Soon after setting sail, a storm lashed at the mighty French fleet. Over 1,300 soldiers and sailors perished in the storm. As the fleet approached Halifax harbor, a dense fog scattered the fleet and they were unable to engage the enemy. The French admiral mysteriously died a short time later, his successor committed suicide, and an unexplainable sickness swept through the fleet, claiming another 1,130 lives. Once the French battle plans were finally drawn, another storm nearly destroyed the fleet again. The final destructive gale forces hit the exact day of a colonial day of prayer and fasting for providential protection against the powerful French fleet. Disgusted and discouraged, the fleet turned in defeat and set sail for France without firing a shot.[2]

The French and Indian War was more than merely a struggle for a geographic empire; it was in part an effort to preserve Biblical Protestantism in America. A French victory would result in a Catholic North America; with a British victory, the land would remain Protestant. A clear illustration of the heated nature of this contest appears in the diary of John Williams, a Puritan preacher from Deerfield, Massachusetts. His town was attacked and leveled by a tribe of Mohawk Indians during Queen Anne's War. Unlike most Mohawks, who were loyal to the Iroquois League and fought for the British, these Mohawks had been converted to Catholicism and fought for the French. According to William's diary, the Indians killed 53 inhabitants of the town and took 111 captives. They then forced the captives to march to Catholic territory in Canada. Those who could not endure the march were killed. Among those killed was Williams's wife.

Once the group arrived in Canada, they were turned over to Jesuit priests, who were even more cruel than the Indians. In the spirit of the Inquisition, they tried almost every method imaginable to force the captives to become Catholics. Of course, the most obvious means, like torture and intimidation, were used. Other methods, however, were more devious. Williams was promised that his three children would be released if he would convert. Others were told that their friends had become Catholics just before dying under Jesuit torture. In spite of these efforts, few actually converted. Despite the physical and mental torture, and despite the fact that he was not allowed to see a copy of the Scriptures, Williams remained faithful. He was eventually rescued by an army from Massachusetts. Although his hardships and losses had been extreme, he still praised the Lord for the experience. He expressed hope that what had happened at Deerfield would serve as a lesson to other colonists of their need to rely on the power and promises of God and to treasure and preserve the Protestant heritage of their homeland. God's hand was directing the entire colonial cause.

God's intervention is once again seen in the 1758 raids of Fort Fontana and Fort Duquesne. Captain John Bradstreet raided Fort Fontana, destroyed the small French navy, confiscated or destroyed all the French artillery, and thus severed the supply lines to the Ohio Valley. This was all done in less than six weeks and without the loss of a single man. Following success with success, the British captured Fort Duquesne later in 1758. This battle, if it can be called a battle at all, marked the turning point of the war. Before the British troops even reached the fort, the French blew it up and retreated. The British then began to rebuild the fort and named it Fort Pitt, which was later renamed Pittsburgh, a city founded on the providence of God.

In 1759, the major battle of the Anglo-French conflict occurred at Quebec, Canada. It determined the future of North America and, consequently, of world progress. "Yet it illustrates not military prowess or human strength, but miscalculations, outright blunders, and poor execution. It is perhaps the clearest example in American history of the fact that a greater power than man directs man's affairs."[3]

Misfortune and miscalculations were hallmarks of this great battle, but only providence could dictate the outcome. Both the French General Marquis de Montcalm and the British Commander James Wolfe committed tactical blunders and both died on the battlefield. When the battle haze cleared, the English Protestant Redcoats captured the fortress and city of Quebec. After nearly nine years of military actions, fighting in North America ceased. The British and her colonies were victorious, and to the victor went the spoils of war.

The peace treaty signed in Paris on February 10, 1763, ceded all lands east of the Mississippi River, not before held, to the English. This was a massive amount of territory which would double the land area of the English colonies. The French also gave up most of their claim to Canada and the West Indies. France's ally, Spain, was also forced to give up its claim of Florida. Half the continent changed hands with the scratch of a pen. North America was now English, but not for long.

The results of the war were drastic and affected the course of history for eternity. First was the massive land exchange. The American colonies were suddenly provided with an immense frontier that was claimed by no European power, only natives. This would lead to greater American exploration, settlement, wealth and independence.

Secondly, Great Britain incurred a great debt during the two-continent war – nearly 82 million pounds, which increased the national debt to 130 million pounds. The interest alone was almost 5 million pounds per year. This enormous debt prompted England to impose oppressive taxes to pay for the colonial conquest. The colonists became bitter over the cruel treatment of the Mother Country. The only remedy after a decade of submitting grievance after grievance to the king was to sever relations with England and endure what was destined to be another war.

The third result of the French and Indian War was the outright blatant British oppression of her American citizens. Colonists were pressed into military service. Private citizens were required to quarter troops in their homes and on their property. The mercantile-driven British crown was manipulating the colonial economy, taxing its populace and suppressing its citizenry. The result was a greater cry for freedom.

Finally, the war brought religious independence. Victory for France in the Americas would have left the colonists under the bondage of Catholicism, but once again, God delivered His "New Israel" to be that light that would spread the gospel to the ends of the earth.

21

The Battle Cry of Freedom

The causes of the American War of Independence are many and complex. The war was far more than the response to a treasonous act of dumping tea in Boston's harbor. It was far more than the act of rebellion by disenchanted colonists toward a cowardly king. The issues that brought about the American Revolution need to be examined in three aspects: economical, legal or moral, and spiritual. Before we examine the reasons for the war, we must define the war itself. Modern historians refer to it as the American Revolution. They point to the colonists as an angry band of rebels seeking to depose the King of England as their legal monarch. Once the bands of the monarchy were dissolved, Americans would be free to establish their own government. In reality, the outlook of the eighteenth century colonists was far from this. In fact, when the colonists referred to the war as a revolution, they meant far less than modern historians read into their actions. Even though a war did ensue, it was very civil. It was not a military or political "bloodletting." There were few atrocities. It was, in reality, a "gentleman's war." The America mindset of the conflict was that it was a war of independence. The July 4, 1776, declaration stated, "We are free." The war that ensued would prove it. Until the declaration, the armed conflict had been in resistance to the high hand of King George. After the declaration, the United States viewed themselves as free from the bondage of the king.

The economic causes of the war were set in place by the original charter and the first permanent settlers of the New World. The British kings chartered the colonies, in essence, to enrich their own empire. Mercantilism dictated that the colony would be solely dependent upon the Mother Country and exist for that purpose. These colonies in the Western Hemisphere were an "invented market" for English goods and services. In time, the colonists developed a deep resentment toward England for her harsh treatment to ensure that the colonies dealt exclusively with English suppliers. The years directly following the French and Indian War witnessed the English Parliament taxation of almost every imaginable colonial consumable item. These taxes were a twofold slap at the colonies. Because the British government was in debt 130 million pounds due to wars with France, the colonists across the Atlantic seemed to be an easy source of tax revenue. After all, the British had defended their interest in America in the French and Indian War (1754-1763). Mercantilism also created high taxes and protective tariffs. Tariffs on non-British goods imported to America protected the king's trade interests. Royal taxes on goods and services in the colonies helped bolster the British treasury for income in the New World.

The colonists viewed tax and tariffs as violations of the King's Charter and protested vehemently. The decade prior to American Independence witnessed the passage of dozens of prohibitive acts upon the colonists. Most of these acts of Parliament were repealed, following colonial protests. But they were all viewed as acts of harassment, one harassment after another in a constant effort to economically oppress loyal American citizens who were subjects of the crown.

Legal and moral issues were a main concern to the colonists, in the years prior to the conflict. The Declaration of Independence states this. The majority of the document is the statement of grievances by the colonists toward the king. The colonies existed by royal charter, issued primarily by the King of England. The grievances state how the monarch had violated his agreement with the colonists. The New England inhabitants especially viewed their role as a "New Israel." God had established a covenant with them, and the King of England was an avenue of fulfilling this godly covenant. Their belief was that human leadership was ordained by God. It was to this end that God administered his Kingdom on earth. The king, being an agent of God, must be subject to Scripture to be obeyed. Therefore, the colonial grievances toward the king were, in reality, notice to the British monarch of his violations of Holy Scripture. For the most part, the colonies were loyal to the king as long as he was loyal to the law, especially the laws of God. "The leaders and the vast majority of the people were steadfastly opposed to the deliberate disruption of law and order, and they were equally opposed to ungodly and unjust laws. Legality in opposition was extremely important."[1]

Many historians attempt to link the two revolutions of the last quarter of the eighteenth century. However, in stark contrast to the French Revolution (1789-1799), the American War of Independence (1775-1783) was based upon the law and the respect for God's law. The differences in the two "revolutions" vary as much as right and wrong, order and disorder, and Americanism and anarchy. The French republic soon gave way to a dictatorship, while the American republic has thrived for over two centuries.

Another point of law argued by the colonists was that their royal charters made them subject only to the King of England, not the English Parliament. Colonial contention was that they were not Englishmen, but Americans ruled by the king. They viewed themselves much like the Welsh or Scots, who had their own legislative bodies but were ruled by the King of England. When King George came to power in 1760, he quickly succumbed to the power of Parliament. It was the Parliament who passed most of the oppressive laws so despised by the colonials. In time, the Americans simply ignored Parliament. This is evident in the Declaration of Independence. Parliament is not directly referred to in the list of grievances, only the king, Thus, when the colonies declared themselves free, they were not declaring their independence from England, for they were never a part of England.

They were declaring their independence from King George.

In their view, King George now had become a tyrant, and as such, forfeited all right he had to their submission. Their views were shaped largely by a work ..., *Vindiciae Contra Tyrannos*, written by an unknown author in 1759. John Adams says that this book was one of the most influential books in America on the eve of war. Among the things set forth in this work are the following, which became guiding principles to the colonists:

a) The ruler cannot command anything contrary to the Law of God. Any ruler who does so seeks to be like God and forfeits his right to the obedience of his subjects.
b) Rebellion is properly defined as a refusal to obey God. To obey the unlawful commands of a ruler is rebellion against God.
c) Resistance against a tyrannical ruler is obedience to God.[2]

The third cause of the War of Independence was a spiritual one. Since man is a spiritual being, this cannot be overlooked. In fact, the true picture of the American Revolution cannot be seen outside of "His story," God's divine plan for man. The roots of the American Revolution lie deep in the Protestant

Reformation. This includes the bravery of Martin Luther, the tenacity of John Knox, the loyalty to Scripture by William Tyndale, and the revolutionary teachings of John Calvin.

> If we call the American statesmen of the late eighteenth century the Founding Fathers of the United States, then the Pilgrims and Puritans were the grandfathers and Calvin the great-grandfather ... Though the fashionable eighteenth century Deism may have pervaded some intellectual circles, the prevailing spirit of Americans before and after the War of Independence was essentially Calvinistic ...[3]

Calvin was an outstanding statesman, but he stood alone as a theologian of the Protestant Reformation. His teachings not only affected theology, but society as well. The American school textbook of the Colonial Period was the Bible, but the textbooks on the Bible were Calvin's voluminous works.

> In colonial America, everyone with the rudiments of schooling knew one book thoroughly: The Bible. And the Old Testament mattered as much as the New. For the American colonies were founded in a time of renewed Hebrew scholarship, and the Calvinistic character of Christian faith in early America emphasized the legacy of Israel ... John Calvin's Hebrew scholarship, and his expounding of the doctrine of sin and human

depravity, impressed the Old Testament aspect of Christianity more strongly upon American than upon European states or other lands where Christians were in the majority.[4]

To understand Calvin's theology brings understanding to America's War of Independence. Calvin taught the absolute sovereignty of God. It was God alone who possessed absolute power. All other power was derived from God. Therefore, the king was subject to God just as the commoner was. God created nations and maintained them by his own hand. This was obvious to eighteenth century Americans, who knew of God's providence at Jamestown, Plymouth, Providence and Quebec.

Calvin also taught the total depravity of man. Therefore, man cannot be trusted since he is sinful. This led to a revival of the covenantal view of civic government. Simply stated, the king was under the authority of the law of God. The government is based upon a contract between the ruler (under divine law) and the people. To act contrary to the contract would be illegal and nullify the contract. Therefore, based upon a Puritanical (Calvinistic) view of godly government, the colonists protested the evils of King George.

The Awakening of the mid-1700's revived the idea that America was that great "New Israel" whose covenant was established with God. Along with this revived "world view" of themselves, colonists believed with confidence that God had ordained their prosperity, and they would prevail no matter the odds or obstacles. Examine the language in the "Declaration of the Cause and Necessity of Taking Up Arms," approved by the Continental Congress on July 6, 1775.

"Our forefathers, inhabitants of the island of Great Britain, left their native land to seek on these shores a residence of civil and religious freedom. At the expense of their blood, at the hazard of their fortunes, without the least charge to the country from which they removed, by unceasing labor and an unconquerable spirit, they effected settlements in the distant and inhospitable wilds of America ... before God and the world, *declare* that, exerting the utmost energy of those powers which our beneficent Creator has graciously bestowed upon us, the arms we have been compelled by our enemies to assume, we will, in defiance of every hazard, with unabating firmness and perseverance, employ for the preservation of our liberties; being with one mind resolved to die free men rather than live slaves.

"With a humble confidence in the mercies of the supreme and impartial Judge and Ruler of the universe, we most devoutly implore His divine goodness to protect us happily through this great conflict, to dispose our adversaries to reconciliation on reasonable terms, and thereby to relieve the empire from the calamities of civil war."[5]

Without the Great Awakening and the revival of the Puritan vision and theology, there would never have been a successful War of Independence in America. It was America's need for a Biblical form of self-government, and her desire for religious freedoms and her willingness to die for both, that brought about the great American dream of "freedom and justice for all."

One would assume that the British victory in the French and Indian War would bring the colonists and the Mother Country closer together. This was far from the truth. The war actually accentuated the need for separation. In 1763, the year the French and Indian War ended, Great Britain established the Proclamation Line. This forbade the colonists to settle beyond the Appalachian Mountains. This act denied the Americans the ability to settle the lands that were specified in their colonial charters. The colonists also felt that they had conquered these lands by defeating the French. Therefore, the lands beyond the Appalachians were doubly theirs and doubly denied by a rogue Parliament.

To further aggravate the situation, the English army remained in the New World. This met with great colonial resistance, since the war was over and there was no need to keep the red-coated army on American soil. The standing army was in violation of the British Petition of Rights (1628), which specified a standing army was to be used only to squelch a rebellion. In 1763, there was no rebellion in America. Two years later, Parliament passed the Quartering Act. This legislation allowed for the army to remain in America and for Americans to house and care for the troops. By authority of Parliament, a British officer could seize an American's home for his own use. Not only could the British soldier commandeer the American house and its contents, but often the householder was relegated to the position of a slave. Often he was exiled from his own home, or even worse. Jonahas Rushdoony states that the British soldier had authority over the entire family, including sexual relations with the women of the house. The Quartering Act was designed to destroy the faith and family of America.[6] Since Americans viewed this as an attack on the family, they had to fight to defend all that was dear to them.

In 1770, violence broke out in Boston. This was a harbinger of war. Loyal colonists of the king were shot and killed by British regular troops for refusing to disperse from a public place. The Boston Massacre became a rallying cry for the colonists in New England, and why not? If British authorities could deny the basic freedom of assembly in Boston, no one would be free. From that point until the independence was secure, Boston became a hot bed of colonial resistance. John and Samuel Adams would fan the flames of independence until the country was ablaze with freedom.

In 1773, the British Parliament passed another tax on goods shipped to America. The Tea Act appeared to be another "royal aggravation," but no more than the dozens of taxes already levied on the colonists. The citizens of Boston rose to the occasion to resist the Tea Tax. On December 16, approximately 6,000 townspeople met for a final appeal to Governor Hutchinson, a representative of the English crown, concerning the unloading of the British-East India tea. The governor refused to hear the citizens. Shrouded by darkness and using disguises, a band of 150 men and boys boarded the three British ships to unload the cargo of tea in the Boston Harbor. Many historians point to this hostile and rebellious act as an outburst of a drunken mob. Other historians refer to the act as "an organized and carefully controlled protest against parliamentary high-handedness."[7] The "rebels" only destroyed the tea. They harmed no British ship man. Following the removal of the tea, the townspeople cleaned the ship and replaced a broken padlock. The action was a planned and peaceful protest of the illegal taxation of loyal subjects of the king.

Charles Fox, a member of the British Parliament, observed the following concerning the conflict with the colonies over taxation:

"A tax can only be laid for three purposes; the first for commercial regulation, the second for revenue, and the third for asserting your right. As to the two first, it had clearly been denied that it is for either; as to the latter, it is only done with a view to irritate and declare war there, which if you [members of Parliament] persist in, I am clearly of the opinion you will effect, or force into open rebellion."[8]

The British Parliament responded to the Boston Tea Party with a series of acts, the Coercive Acts, subjugating American citizens in every way possible. First, the Port of Boston was closed until the $75,000 value of the tea was paid. Other legislative acts reduced the power of the Massachusetts colony and increased the authority of the British officials in the colony. The colonists referred to the series of legislation as "The Intolerable Acts." Each was another illegal lash by Parliament toward the colonists of New England. Since the colonies were chartered by the king and the king only, Parliament should have no rule over them, they insisted. The colonies had their own legislatures. In their opinion, they were not bound by Parliament.

The final act of British legislative aggression was the Quebec Act of 1774. This established the Roman Catholic Church as the state church of the province. Further, the act expanded the territory of Quebec to the Ohio River, thereby annulling colonial claims to the Ohio Valley Region and encircling the Protestant colonies with Catholicism. The colonies immediately protested on the grounds of the violation of the colonial charters and the God-given rights to worship one's God as he sees fit. What greater insult could be issued than for a Protestant Parliament to establish a Catholic religion in America? The colonists realized that if Parliament could establish Catholicism in Quebec, it could also legislate Anglicanism as the state church for the other thirteen colonies. This would lead to the destruction of all dissenting churches in America.

The colonial response to the suppressive acts of Parliament was almost always peaceable and legal.

Colonists viewed King George as an under-shepherd of God. Any grievances must be presented in a loyal and respectful Christian way. In the past, when the colonists resisted the intolerable English legislation, Parliament would retract the suppressive laws. Therefore, as late as 1774, many Americans saw little need for separation from England.

To fan the small flame for independence, zealots such as Samuel Adams developed a system of informing the citizenry in and around Boston. His Committee of Correspondence kept information flowing about Parliament's exploitation of Bostonians. Soon, each colony had its own committee to alert its townspeople to be aware of British intervention in their colony's affairs. These Committees of Correspondence helped pave the way for a Continental Congress to meet in September of 1774. This congress was the first representative body to meet with delegates from each colony. The majority of delegates present were favorable toward settling grievances with England. Only the most radical representatives called for an open and outright break with the Mother Country. On October 14, 1774, a Declaration of Resolves was passed by Congress. This document asserted the rights of the colonies, while recognizing only limited authority of Parliament. In sending this declaration to King George, the colonists were firmly stating their loyalty to the crown and reproach for Parliament. However, British response did not come from the king or from Parliament. In six months, the British regulars would be firing on the king's subjects again.

22

The Shot Heard Around the World

To understand the American War of Independence, one must be aware of the prelude to war. The Declaration of Independence was penned in July 1776, at the third meeting of the Continental Congress. By then, the English had been harassing her colonies for years, with both legislative and military aggression. The early colonial period had been an unprecedented time of moral, civil, and religious freedom in the colonies. These freedoms were based largely upon the laws and customs of each separate colony. For nearly a century-and-a-half, religious freedoms flourished, especially in the North. This was the foundation of the colonial experience – freedom.

The French and Indian War upset the balance of liberty in America in the 1760s. England, the mother country, was deeply in debt due to a series of wars in Europe and America. Parliament looked at her colonies in America as an added source of tax revenue to help fund the costly act of war. For over a decade following the French and Indian War, the British Parliament passed a series of laws to extract exorbitant taxes from their colonies in America. These taxes, along with a prohibition on colonial development westward, fostered tension in the quickly developing colonies. In 1770, there were armed conflicts in New York and Boston. The Boston Massacre led to bloodshed, killing five Bostonians and wounding another six. As tension heightened, the imperial tyranny did as well.

In 1773, the Boston Tea Party was an armed, orderly statement to the British crown that Bostonians had had enough of his lawless taxation and infringements into their commercial lives. With each new tyrannical tax, the colonies would firmly reply with a list of grievances for the unlawful taxation. As time passed and tensions soared, the grievances were longer and came with more force and resolve. Even the wealthy planters of Virginia finally joined the beleaguered merchants of Massachusetts in a call for regress or revolution (The Fairfax County Resolves and The Suffolk County Resolves, respectively).

In September 1774, once again the British army lashed out in aggression against the colonial citizenry by seizing the Charlestown, Massachusetts arsenal. It was time to unite. The Sons of Liberty in Boston and New York united in Committees of Correspondence to herald the clarion call for freedom. Political treatises were circulated through this network of committees all along the eastern seaboard. The first Continental Congress met in October of 1774 to discuss grievances against the king and unity among the colonies. On December 14 of that year, patriots took the offensive.

> Warned by Paul Revere of a British plan to station troops at Portsmouth, New Hampshire, a group of Massachusetts militiamen led by Major John Sullivan successfully attack the arsenal of Fort William and Mary in Portsmouth and capture arms and ammunition. No lives are lost in this encounter.[1]

Even when the colonists acted with force, it was to defend their basic rights.

The British Parliament and military, embarrassed by the Portsmouth capture, responded the following year. On February 9, 1775, the British Parliament declared the Massachusetts colony to be in a state of rebellion. The following happened on April 14:

> Massachusetts Governor Gage receives a letter from Lord Dartmouth ordering him to use all necessary force to implement the Coercive and other acts, and to strike preemptively to circumvent further buildup of the colonial military machine.[2]

The military governor, General Thomas Gage, quickly took the initiative on April 18 by marching on Lexington. Primarily, he hoped to seize militia arms stored in the towns of Lexington and Concord. He also hoped to arrest two pesky colonial patriots, Samuel Adams and John Hancock. The two were having dinner at the home of Reverend Jonas Clark. Clark was a member of the so-called "Black Regiment." These were ministers who openly preached liberty and militarily trained their parishioners to defend themselves against the armed aggression of the British. Clark, a Lexington minister, had been training men of his church for months. While Reverend Clark was entertaining the two members of the notorious "Sons of Liberty," Paul Revere and William Dawes were frantically riding to inform the citizenry that the "British are coming!"

On the morning of April 19, 1775, the British regulars arrived on the village green of the hamlet of Lexington. Nineteenth century historian George Bancroft tells the story of the bravery of the Lexingtonians.

> 'At two in the morning, under the eye of the minister [Rev. Jonas Clark], and of [John] Hancock and [Samuel] Adams, Lexington common was alive with the minute-men; and not with them only, but with the old men, who were exempts, except in case of immediate danger to the town. The roll was called, and, of militia and alarm men, about one hundred and thirty answered to their names. The captain, John Parker, ordered every one to load with powder and ball, but to take care not to be the first to fire.'

Bancroft adds: 'The ground on which they trod was the altar of freedom, and they were to furnish the victims.'

Speaking of the Lexington Church in Massachusetts, Bancroft observed, 'How often had they, with renewed professions of their faith, looked up to God as the stay of their fathers and the protector of their privileges!'[3]

When the immaculately clad Redcoats assembled to disperse the band of rag tag farmers and merchants who had been trained in the art of warfare by Parson Clark, the patriot Captain Parker started to dismiss his outnumbered band. Then shots rang out. "For a century and a half, Christians had been stepping over that parade ground on their way to church for worship. Now they were defending their right to continue to worship freely."[4]

By the time the firing was over, ten Americans were wounded and eight were dead, with only one British casualty. Even though the skirmish lasted but a few minutes, the die was cast. War had begun. The minutemen would be immortalized and their leader's word would become prophetic. Captain John Parker calmly stated before hostilities began, "Don't fire unless fired upon, but if they want a war, let it begin here." Thus, the shot fired on the village green at Lexington was a "shot heard around the world." The War of Independence, in essence, started over a year before the Declaration of Independence was drafted. By this act of tyranny, the invasion force of British regulars was dispatched to confiscate private property from the subjects of the king. The citizenry of Massachusetts simply viewed their actions as defending themselves and their property from a monarch in rebellion to the authority of God.

The British troops proceeded on to Concord to seize munitions and supplies. Suddenly, Minutemen appeared to defend their property and homes. The British had gone too far. Americans would stand and fight for basic freedoms and independence. Fight they did, attacking the British as they retired back to Boston.

> From that point on, they were running the bloodiest gauntlet that British troops had ever experienced-or would experience until the Light Brigade charged at Balaklava. All along the way, the Minutemen kept up a steady fire on their flanks, well-concealed behind stone walls, hedges, and screening woods. The increasingly frustrated British hardly ever saw more than a dozen in one body. The Minutemen would take cover ahead of them, aiming carefully and firing, reloading while lying down, and then running ahead to get in another shot. Finally, the British were forced to send out large bodies of flankers to sweep the woods and fields on either side of the road. Now the Minutemen began to take casualties too. But the flankers, who had to push through underbrush and ford creeks, quickly

tired and had difficulty keeping ahead of the column.[5]

Two months after the initial battle of the war, the patriots dug in to defend their homes against another invasion of trained British regular troops. The British attacked at Bunker Hill (some insist it was Breed's Hill), just outside Boston. Once again, the untrained colonial troops were forced to withdraw, but this time they inflicted twice as many casualties as they incurred. The Americans were building resolve, but they needed a leader. In June of 1775, Congress made provision to raise an army and appointed the hero of the French and Indian War, George Washington, as commander-in-chief.

Who was this 43-year-old military hero? He was a native Virginian with little education, no formal military training and only brief service in public life. He married into wealth and had no children of his own. He was a surveyor by trade and a veteran of the French and Indian War by necessity. His distinguished military service to the king placed him first in the minds of the Continental Congress, who elected him unanimously to be commander of the Continental forces. Washington was more than a chance war hero. He was a man of substance. He was a well-disciplined, practical man with a deep and abiding faith in God.

> George Washington was truly a great man by everyone's reckoning. His character was remarkable, if we are to believe the judgment of his contemporaries:

Patrick Henry said: '[I]f you speak of solid information and sound judgment, Washington is unquestionably the greatest man of them all.'

Leading American historian of the 19th century George Bancroft said of Washington: '[H]is qualities were so faultlessly proportioned that the whole people rather claimed him as its choicest representative, the most complete expression of all its attainments and aspirations.'

Thomas Jefferson observed: 'His integrity was the most pure, his justice the most inflexible I have ever known ... no motives of interest of consanguinity, of friendship or hatred, being able to bias his decision.'

And so Bancroft could conclude: 'Wherever he became known, in his family, his neighborhood, his country, his native state, the continent, the camp, civil life, among the common people in foreign courts, throughout the civilized world, and even among the savages, he beyond all other men had the confidence of his kind.'[6]

Upon taking command of the Continental forces, the humble Washington wrote to his wife, Martha: "I hope my undertaking this service is designed to answer some good purpose. I rely confidently on that Providence which has heretofore preserved and been bountiful to me."[7] His moral fiber seems to be a product of self-discipline and practical Christianity, which he developed from his youth. Notice two of his first orders given in July, just days after assuming command.

> "The General most earnestly requires and expects a due observance of those articles of war established for the government of the Army which forbid profane cursing, swearing and drunkenness. And in like matter he requires and expects of all officers and soldiers not engaged in actual duty, a punctual attendance of Divine services, to implore the blessing of Heaven upon the means used for our safety and defense.
>
> "The General orders this day to be religiously observed by the forces under his Command, exactly in the manner directed by the Continental Congress. It is therefore strictly enjoined on all officers and soldiers to attend Divine service. And it is expected that all those who go to worship do take their arms, ammunition and accouterments and are prepared for immediate action, if called upon."[8]

Washington was far more than a Deist in belief. He was a dedicated Christian, who believed that God would providentially care for His people. With no army, no navy, no money, or even a unified country, George Washington humbly accepted the formidable challenge before him, to take on the most powerful nation on the face of the earth. How could the genteel Virginian take on such a task? The American commander wrote of his inner strength in a book of prayers when he was about 20 years old.

This was God's chosen man for America's greatest need. In this time of crisis, Washington brought both fear and fight to the battlefield. His fear of the Almighty was foremost. The fear of failure, America's extension, and personal loss were always secondary. The great general's fight was always overshadowed by his fearful respect for God as well. Washington won no tactical battles, was seldom superior in force, and never over-powered the British invaders. What he did, he did with God's blessing, power and strength. A survey of the six years of conflict is a testimony of God's grace and providence, and Washington's faith and trust. He was Commander in Chief, serving under the King of Kings and Lord of Lords.

23

No King But Jesus

In October 1775, British forces burned the town of Falmouth, Maine in retaliation. One act of aggression followed another. But, the fledgling colonies showed resolve and fortitude. To this point, the conflict had been a New England affair whipped to a fever pitch by patriots like The Sons of Liberty. Boston was the hub of the "rebellion," and British regulars operated primarily to root out insurrection there.

In November, the Royal Governor of Virginia declared martial law in his state, and began to raise a loyalist army to put down the rebels of the Old Dominion. In December, he was defeated at the Battle of Great Bridge by a force of 900 Virginia and Carolina militia. In January the governor ordered his loyalist troops to fire on other Virginians at Norfolk. The state experienced its first civil war in 1775-1776. By this point, there was no way to stop an outright war. The two largest and most influential colonies were now arming themselves in opposition to their own king. In reality, Americans were a country without a king. This was totally foreign to them. Since 1607, America had been ruled by a monarch. The colonists had enjoyed the distance of the New World while, at the same time, claiming allegiance to the British crown. By 1775, the majority of Englishmen in America realized they were really Americans with an English heritage. King George III had violated his obligations to his colonies, thereby leaving them free to govern themselves. Freedom had become too sweet for Americans. They would return to the vision of their founders, to follow God. They no longer needed a tyrannical king or a suppressive Parliament.

The spiritual awakening of the colonies in the first half of the century, coupled with the military success of the second half, charted a course of freedom for the American colonies. Only one thing stood in their way: the king. Since the dawn of American colonialism, English mercantilism had bound the colonies to the mother country. But, by the third quarter of the eighteenth century, industrious Americans could foresee the severing of many of the ties that bound them. With the heavy-handedness of Parliament, Americans were looking for other avenues to survive without their overbearing mother.

The plan was simple. Washington and Mason outlined it in the Fairfax Resolves: Develop our own trades and crafts and when we are self-sufficient, cut all ties with Great Britain. The crown supplied no necessary trade, protection, or service to the colonies. Americans could and should be independent. The main problem was not independence, for in real terms the colonies were very close to being independent from their inception. The commercial ties with the mother country were all that preserved the union by 1775. Many Americans struggled with the Scriptural reason for independence. After all, had not most of the original colonies come to the continent believing it was God's will for the king to allow them to come? Were not the colonies all chartered by a God-ordained charter, granted by the crown? The haunting question in 1775 was, "Is there a Biblical mandate for declaring independence from a God-ordained monarch?" The answer was in the tyranny of the crown..

For a decade, British monarchs had inflicted undue and unjust legislation upon their colonies in America.

"When does tyranny become tyranny?

"By Scripture, it happens when a ruler breaks the commandment of 2 Samuel 23:3 (KJV): *He that ruleth over men must be just, ruling in the fear of God."*

"By Puritan interpretation, constructed before the first Pilgrims and Puritans embarked for America, it is when a ruler knowingly and deliberately contravenes the will of God, thus making it impossible for his subjects to follow that divine will.

"By the Magna Carta, which established English common law, it is when a ruler ceases to act under that law and denies his subjects their rights, as guaranteed by that law.

"By pronouncement of James I: 'A king ceases to be a king, and degenerates to a tyrant, as soon as he leaves off to rule according to his laws.'

"By Parliamentary interpretation, it is when Englishmen have measures imposed upon them, such as taxation, without their consent or even representation.

"By every one of these definitions, James II's attitude toward the Colonies was tyrannical. As the Puritans saw it, *he* was the rebel, for he was using the power of his office, not to serve the people but to oppress them. Therefore he was in direct disobedience to the will of God, as delineated in both Testaments of the Bible."[1]

Englishmen and Americans alike understood tyranny. After all, was this not the reason for going to a new world, for braving the seas and placing oneself in peril of starvation and Indian annihilation? Was it not to avoid the tyrants of England, Holland, Spain or France? Did not the Pilgrims sail to Holland just to avoid the suppressive King of England and his jealous religious henchman, the Bishop of Canterbury? The Puritans could not purify the church, so they sought a new land. Who was behind the abuses of the indulgences of the Anglican Church? It was none other than the king himself. Baptists had been martyred for centuries at the hands of infidels who sat on the throne of England. French Huguenots were chased from their homelands by their own wicked monarchs.

Even the Catholics had felt the persecution of English kings and sought a better land in America.

For a century, American pulpits decried absolutism of the monarchs, while they exalted a God of law and order. For example, in the late 1600s, the Puritan Increase Mather boldly stated the following:

> "To submit and resign their charter would be inconsistent with the main end of their fathers' coming to New England ... [Although resistance would provoke] great sufferings, [it was] better to suffer than sin. (Hebrews 11:26, 27). Let them put their trust in the God of their fathers, which is better than to put confidence in princes. And if they suffer, because they dare not comply with the wills of men against the will of God, they suffer in good cause and will be accounted martyrs in the next generation, and at the great day."[2]

During the interlude of the spiritual awakening and the war with France, Reverend Jonathan Mayhew of Boston preached fervently against the abuse of God-given powers of government. He railed against the obstinate monarch who would neglect or inflict his providentially appointed subjects.

> "It is blasphemy to call tyrants and oppressors God's ministers...When [magistrates] rob and ruin the public, instead of being guardians of its peace and welfare, they immediately cease to be the ordinance and ministers of God, and

no more deserve that glorious character than common pirates and highwaymen."³

In colonial America, both absolute monarchs and the exaltation of a God of law and order existed. But for 150 years, the divine right of kings did not interfere with the divine leadership of God. This all changed once the king needed money, following the French and Indian War. Americans may have been out of the reach of the bishop or even the king, but not the tax collector. The crown and Parliament saw the colonists as debtors, and by 1764, it was time to pay up.

Some Americans quickly realized the king had crossed the line of tyranny, while for others it took a war to convince them. But by 1775, the country was awakened to the cry that "taxation without representation is tyranny." But all through her history, American pulpits had been ablaze with the gospel of liberty, much like Mayhew's pulpit in Boston.

> The king is as much bound by his oath not to infringe the legal rights of the people, as the people are bound to yield subjection to him. From whence it follows that as soon as the prince sets himself up above the law, he loses the king in the tyrant. He does, to all intents and purposes, unking himself by acting out of and beyond that sphere which the constitution allows him to move in, and in such cases he has no more right to be obeyed than any inferior officer who acts beyond his commis-

sion. The subject's obligation to allegiance then ceases, of course, and to resist him is no more rebellion than to resist any foreign invader...it is making use of the means, and the only means, which God has put into their power for mutual and self-defense.[4]

Robert Trent Paine, a signer of the Declaration of Independence and former attorney-general of the United States, called Jonathan Mayhew, "The Father of the Civil and Religious Liberty in Massachusetts and America."[5] Mayhew clearly called Bostonians to follow the God of the Scriptures over the rulers of man.

"To say that subjects in general are not proper judges when their governors oppress them, and play the tyrant; and when they defend their rights, administer justice impartially, and promote the public welfare, is as great treason as ever man uttered; - 'tis treason, - not against one single man, but the state – against the whole body politic; - 'tis treason against mankind; - 'tis treason against common sense; - 'tis treason against God. And this impious principle lays the foundation for justifying all the tyranny and oppression that ever any prince was guilty of."[6]

So common was the call for Godly government that sermons were regularly preached on the subject. "Election sermons," as they were called, focused on man's responsibility to elect godly officials and the officials' responsibility to remain a true Christian leader.

It was in the so-called "Election Sermons" of Massachusetts, Connecticut, New Hampshire, and Vermont that the ministers expressed themselves most fluently on the subject of civil government. According to the Rev. William Gordon of Roxbury, an historian of the Revolution: 'Two sermons have been preached annually for a length of time, the one on general election day, the last Wednesday in May, when the new general court has been used to meet, according to charter, and elect counselors for the ensuing year; the other, some little while after, on the artillery election day, when the officers are re-elected, or new officers chosen. On these occasions political subjects are deemed very proper; but it is expected that they be treated in a decent, serious, and instructive manner...The sermon is styled the *Election Sermon* and is printed. Every representative has a copy for himself, and generally one or more for the minister or ministers of his town. As the patriots have prevailed, the preachers of each sermon have been the zealous friends of liberty; and the passages most adapted to promote the spread and love of it have been selected and circulated far and wide by means of newspapers.[7]

In addition to expounding the Scriptures, New England ministers would cite Christian statesmen and philosophers on the subject of government as it intersected with religion. John Locke, John Milton, Baron Montesquieu and William Blackstone, all of whom were Christians, contributed heavily to the highly educated ministers' sermons of the eighteenth century pulpits of America. Law, philosophy, culture and Biblical Christianity all filtered down from the churches of America to weave the fabric of its moral and social fiber.

When America came to the crossroads of independence, she began to understand from her pulpits that the Bible decries tyrannical lordship over men, and by 1775, the pews of America's churches were filled with the doctrines of moral responsibility and civil liberty. Therefore, when the king was out of control, the issue of obedience to tyranny was out of the subjects' hands. They could not exercise their God-given responsibilities to follow the king. Though taxation was an issue, the greater problem was the underlying issue of tyranny. The Christians of America understood this. That is why their battle cry was not only "Taxation without representation is tyranny." It was a far deeper cry, a more noble cry, and a cry from the heart. The true battle cry of freedom during the war was "No king but King Jesus."

24

In the Course of Human Events

—⚎—

Not only has the history of American Independence been different, it has been different by design. The War of Independence was just that, a war that came as a result of America's declaration of this independence. It never was a rebellion. For a decade preceding the declaration, Americans pled with the king concerning their rights and grievances. In 1775, colonists, Americans, had been fired upon. American blood had been shed on American soil, defending America. The British had gone too far. Lexington, Concord and Bunker Hill seemed to be a call for all Americans to defend their homes, freedoms and native lands.

Some refer to the Colonial War with Britain as the American Revolution. It is true that many of our Founding Fathers used this terminology. However, the founders meant far less than do contemporary historians, who attempt to equate the French Revolution with the American Revolution. In respect to the French bloodletting, the American "revolt" was somewhat pale and disappointing. The results were the same in that both revolutions "brought forth a new nation," but the American Republic has been far more lasting. When the American independence was won, a republic was established that exists today. Our French counterpart is on its seventh government since their revolt ended in 1799.

What set the revolutions apart? The French revolutionaries started with an amoral view of man and an atheistic view of God, and built a nation without a consideration for morals or God. The American Republic was wrought from a revolution based upon a covenantal relationship with God, based on charters by the British king. These charters were grossly neglected and constantly violated. The colonies presented their grievances to the British crown many times. King George III had continually rejected the colonial petitions. The Americans entered war based upon the idea that they had exhausted every possible avenue of avoiding armed conflict. The French willingly went to war to overthrow a monarch. The Americans fought for God-given freedoms deprived by the British monarchy. The French overthrew their government. The Americans won their independence.

The acts that precipitated war further illustrate that the American "revolution" was not born in malicious rebellion.

1. The colonies presented their grievances to the king as loyal, honorable subjects of the crown.
2. The colonies acted in respect to the law, and with respect to personal property. This is evidenced in the Boston Tea Party and echoed in the Fairfax County Resolves.
3. The peaceable resistance to the king's representatives illustrates a non-rebellious spirit in America.
4. The Christian nature of America seemed to call for reconciliation with the King of England instead of rebellion against him.
5. When armed conflict occurred in 1775, the British were the aggressors. The colonists only defended their property.

The American colonies exhausted almost every conceivable avenue of reconciliation with the mother country. Therefore, by 1776, the only logical course seemed to be independence. The patriot networks, such as the Sons of Liberty, had been fanning the flames of freedom for quite some time. The Committees of Correspondence had circulated patriotic leaflets and pamphlets throughout the colonies, while the Committees of Public Safety served as state bodies to warn the people of impending aggression by the British Redcoats. The first Continental Congress of the thirteen colonies assembled in September 1774. They discussed their need of unification, but most delegates were hopeful of the prospects of remaining loyal to the crown. On April 18, the British marched on Lexington to seize munitions from the citizens. By the end of the next day, several Americans lay dead on the streets of Lexington and Concord, Massachusetts, and for all practical purposes, war had begun.

By that time, most of the delegates to the second Continental Congress had been selected for the May 10 assembly in Philadelphia. Noticeably, the tone of the 1775 session was more somber and deliberate than the previous year. In late April, the Massachusetts Provincial Congress ordered the mobilization of over 13,000 soldiers, and requested the aid of other colonies. By the end of May, colonial militia had snatched Fort Ticonderoga and Crown Point from the British hands, and seemed ready to defend the New England colonies from further English aggression. On June 12, General Gage imposed martial law in Massachusetts, declaring all armed colonists to be traitors and in rebellion against the king.

In response, the Continental Congress appropriated funds for salaries for six companies of soldiers, and appointed George Washington as general of the Continental Army. In light of their present danger, the Congress acted both to defend themselves and to reconcile with King George. On July 5, the American body passed an "Olive Branch Petition," expressing hopes to the English monarch that their differences could be settled by diplomacy instead of bloodshed. The following day, Congress rejected the idea of independence by passing the Declaration of the Causes and Necessities of Taking Up Arms. This declaration called for colonial resistance to British aggression, but not for independence. King George rejected the conciliatory Olive Branch Petition of the Continental Congress on August 23, 1775. He went further toward war by proclaiming the thirteen American colonies to be in an outright and open state of rebellion against the crown. The colonies had no choice but to fully arm themselves and prepare for war with the most powerful nation on Earth, their mother land, England.

The American backs were against the wall. Would the outcome be a fight for freedom, or a firing squad for rebellion? 1776 would be the long, agonizing year of decision, but for many Americans, the decision was already made. Virginians like Richard Henry Lee and Patrick Henry had already cast their lot for liberty. Lee, a devout Christian, was a member of the first Committee of Correspondence in Virginia. He was valuable in attaining intelligence reports from England through his brother, Arthur Lee, who lived in London. Lee, the Virginian, undoubtedly believed in independence before most of the other patriots, due in part to his London connection. It would be Lee that took the lead in the battle cry for freedom.

Patrick Henry was also a committed Christian. His oratory stirred Virginians to action with declarations like the following one from the Virginia Provincial Convention meeting at the House of Burgesses in Richmond.

> "For [my] own part [I] consider it as nothing less than a question of freedom or slavery…It is only in this way that we can hope to arrive

at truth, and fulfill the great responsibility which we hold to God and our country...Sir, we have done everything that could be done to avert the storm which is now coming on. We have petitioned; we have remonstrated; we have supplicated; we have prostrated ourselves before the throne, and have implored its interposition to arrest the tyrannical hands of the ministry and parliament. Our petitions have been slighted; our remonstrances have produced additional violence and insult; our supplications have been disregarded; and we have been spurned, with contempt...We must fight! I repeat it, sir, we must fight! An appeal to arms and to the God of Hosts is all that is left us!...

"Sir, we are not weak, if we make a proper use of the means which the God of nature hath placed in our power. Three millions of people, armed in the Holy cause of liberty, and in such a country as that which we possess, are invincible by any force which our enemy can send against us.

"Besides, sir, we shall not fight our battle alone. There is a just God who presides over the destinies of nations, and who will raise up friends to fight our battle for us. The battle, sir, is not to the strong alone; it is to the vigilant, the active, the brave...Is life so dear or peace so sweet as to be purchased at the price of chains and slavery? Forbid it, Almighty God! I know not what course others may take; but as for me, give me liberty or give me death!"[1]

Henry's faith in the providential care of God for the colonies is evident as he reminds Virginians that God will also "raise up friends" to aid the American cause.

The year 1776 dawned very bleakly in America. War, though undeclared, was imminent. But who would stand for their liberties? It was believed that a vast majority of the American populace was still loyal to the king who had labeled them rebels. Many colonies felt that they had no need to arm, for the fight was not theirs. Only Massachusetts had been fired upon. Only parts of Virginia and North Carolina had called for independence, while other parts of the same colony were very loyal to the king. Pennsylvania seemed to be opposed to independence in early 1776, while New York was indifferent to the issue. B. J. Lossing, the nineteenth century historian, notes the philosophical climate of 1776.

> An aspiration for political independence was not a prevailing sentiment among the people of the Anglo-American colonies, until about the commencement of the year 1776. It had indeed been a favorite idea with a very few of the early leaders in the political movements antecedent to, and productive of, the War of the Revolution; yet manifest expediency, and

a lingering hope of obtaining justice from the mother country, and through it reconciliation, caused them to confine the audible expression of this sentiment to the private circle of tried friendship. Samuel Adams, Richard Henry Lee, Patrick Henry, Timothy Dwight, and a few others had indeed breathed the subject in the ears of their countrymen, but the idea met with little favor, even among the most ardent patriots.[2]

In March, the Continental Congress acted on the troublesome issue of loyalty. The body passed a resolution recommending a policy of disarming all colonists who were loyal to King George. In May, the Virginia delegation to the Congress was empowered by the legislature of the colony to push for independence, but for many, the idea was still unthinkable. Then the assembly of Rhode Island directed its inhabitants to redirect their oath of allegiance to the colony and not the king.

By the middle of 1776, the fate of the country changed drastically and very quickly.

On the fourteenth of June, a special assembly was called in Connecticut, and a resolution was adopted, by a unanimous vote, instructing the delegates of that colony in the General Congress, to 'give their assent to a declaration of independence…'

On the fifteenth of June, the representatives of New Hampshire unanimously instructed their delegates to join the other colonies in this question. On the twenty-first of the same month, new delegates...of New Jersey, and they were instructed, 'in case they judged it necessary and expedient for supporting the just rights of America, to join in declaring the united colonies independent, and entering into a confederation for union and defence.'

The assembly of Pennsylvania, held in June, removed the restrictions laid upon their delegates...The convention of Maryland positively forbade, by a resolution passed about the last of May, their delegates voting for independence. Georgia and Delaware left their representatives free to act without any instructions or restrictions.[3]

While it appeared a majority of the members of the Continental Congress favored separation from Great Britain, Britain was still great. Anyone who had taken up arms or who had aided those who had were considered rebels by powerful King George, and anyone who dared to openly state his independence on a formal declaration, would be guilty of treason and punishable by death!

While a majority of the members of the Congress were yearning, with anxious and irrepressible zeal, for the consummation of an event which they felt must inevitably occur-and all eyes were turned with earnest gaze upon that August assembly as the organ that should proclaim 'liberty to the land, and to the inhabitants thereof,' there seemed to be no one courageous enough to step forth and take the awful responsibility of lifting the knife that should sever the cord that bound the American colonies to the British throne. It was very properly apprehended, that the person who should first propose to declare the colonies independent, would be specially marked by the royal government as an arch rebel, and that no effort would be spared to quench his spirit or bring his person to the scaffold. In that dark hour of hesitation and fearful dread, Richard Henry Lee, of Virginia, assumed the perilous responsibility of presenting to Congress a proposition to dissolve all political connection with Great Britain...On the seventh of June, Mr. Lee moved the resolution, 'That these united colonies are, and of right ought to be free and independent states; and that all political connection between them and the state of Great Britain is, and ought to be, totally dissolved.'[4]

The discussion on the resolution for independence was postponed until July 1, when it was to be considered by the entire Congress. In the meantime, a committee was appointed to draft a formal declaration. Thomas Jefferson, Benjamin Franklin,

John Adams, Roger Sherman, and Robert Livingston constituted the committee entrusted with drafting the document. By July 1, the American course was set. All that remained was to stay the course.

> When intelligence reached America that the King had declared the colonists *rebels* — that thousands of German troops had been engaged by Parliament to come hither to assist in the work of subjugating a people struggling for right and justice — and that the British government was collecting all its mighty energies, for the purpose of striking a blow of such intensity as to scatter into fragments every vestige of the rightful claims of the colonists, to enjoy the prerogatives granted to them by Magna Carta, a deep and solemn conviction seized the minds of the people, that the last ray of hope of reconciliation had faded away, and that unbending resistance or absolute slavery was the only alternative left them. The bonds of filial affection were rudely severed by the unnatural parent and the deserted and outlawed children were driven by necessity to seek shelter beneath a palladium of their own construction.[5]

The committee, chaired by the red-headed Thomas Jefferson, responded with a preliminary draft of the Declaration of Independence on June 28. It was debated, altered and amended until the fourth of July, when it was voted upon. Although the individual vote by the delegates on the acceptance of the declaration was not unanimous, the vote of the colonies was. All 13 voted for independence, and thereby declared the colonies free and independent states.

The preamble of the declaration expressed the heartfelt desire of the American people to express their beliefs to the world concerning their independence. In the opening paragraph of the Declaration of Independence, the document recognizes the existence and interaction of God in the affairs of man. This perspective is from the Puritan's covenant theology, the bedrock of American faith. The British crown had violated his covenant with the colonists. The colonists boldly stated that they must continue in this covenant with God to establish a new nation based upon godly principles, one that the "laws of nature and of nature's God entitle them." The declaration openly recognized God as man's creator and sustainer. Also, man's basic "unalienable rights," such as "life, liberty, and the pursuit of happiness," were guaranteed by the Creator and should be protected by the government.

> ...when the Declaration was debated before Congress, they added the phrase, 'appealing to the Supreme Judge of the World, for the rectitude of our intentions,' as well as the words 'with a firm reliance on the protection of divine Providence.' Most of the revisions of Jefferson's original work had to do with the Lord. Thus we see the Continental Congress

declaring to all the world their Christian convictions.[6]

The main body of the document enumerates the 27 specific grievances against the king and his agents. The authors of the declaration, Thomas Jefferson in particular, are careful not to mention parliament by name. Parliament had not been mentioned in the original colonial charters granted by James I and played no part in any of the charters granted to the other colonies. The colonists justly believed that because King George had violated his inherited monarchial agreement of the original colonial charters, the colonies should enjoy all the rights of Englishmen. The colonists felt that George had proven himself a tyrant "unfit to be the ruler of a free people." Having made every possible attempt at reconciliation, America had no recourse but to sever its ties with Great Britain.

On July 4, 1776, the English colonies shook themselves free from the tyranny of the British Empire and declared themselves to be free Americans. Was this an act of arrogance or an act of providence? John Adams shares his belief: "I always consider the settlement of America with reverence and wonder, as the opening of a grand scheme and design in Providence for the illumination and emancipation of the slavish part of mankind all over the earth."[7]

With a stroke of the pen, Americans declared themselves free from Britain. Were they? What ensued for the next five years was the War of Independence. Americans were fighting because they were free to protect their lives, their fortunes and their sacred honor. In respect to the patriots of the American Revolution, they were not in a revolt against Britain. They had firmly and peaceably presented their grievances to the king, and with Scripture, they had presented their case. George had repeatedly allowed Parliament to subject his subjects to suppressive treatment. Therefore, the colonies declared themselves free and were willing to fight for that precious freedom.

The idea of "one nation under God" was a political axiom rooted in the Great Awakening, based upon the Puritan experience, founded in Calvinism and derived from the Bible. The American experience has as its bedrock, the Bible. The nation was founded upon Scripture, because the founders were Christian. Foundational documents, founders' diaries and fundamental governmental dealings all attest to the deity of Jehovah and His relationship to his New Israel, America. Is it any wonder that when King George violated his covenantal agreement with the colonies, that the colonists appealed to a higher authority, that of King Jesus? This sense of destiny had become a voice of prophecy in a South Carolina courtroom in April 1776. South Carolina Supreme Court Justice William Henry Drayton uttered these words.

> "I think it my duty to declare, in the awful seat of justice, and before Almighty God, that in my opinion, the Americans can have no safety, but by divine favor, their own virtues, and their being so prudent, as not to leave it in the power of British rulers to

injure them. Indeed, the ruinous and deadly injuries received on our side, and the jealousies entertained, and which in the nature of things must daily increase against us, on the other, demonstrate to a mind the least given to reflection, that true reconcilement can never exist between Great Britain and America, the latter being subject to the former... The Almighty created America to be independent of Great Britain: let us beware of the impiety of being backward to act as instruments in the Almighty hand, now extended to accomplish his purpose, and by the completion of which, alone, America, in the nature of human affairs, can be secure against the crafty and insidious designs of her enemies, who think her favor and prosperity already by far too great. In a word, our piety and political safety are so blended, that to refuse our labor in this divine work, is to refuse to be a great, a free, a pious and a happy people."[8]

After affirming the Declaration of Independence with a formal vote on July 4, 1776, the delegates to the Continental Congress re-assembled on August 2 to sign the final draft. This was a solemn occasion as each was called to step forward and affix his signature and thereby possibly sign his own death warrant. The Bostonian John Adams contemplated that day.

"If it be the pleasure of Heaven that my country shall require the poor offering of my life, the victim shall be ready, at the appointed hour of sacrifice, come when that hour may. But while I do live, let me have a country, and that a free country!"[9]

After signing the document with unusually large and exact penmanship, John Hancock broke the monumental silence of the moment by declaring, "His majesty can now read my name without glasses, and he can also double the price on my head. We must be unanimous; there must be no pulling different ways; we must all hang together."[10] Benjamin Franklin, the sage from Philadelphia, smugly responded, "Yes, we must indeed all hang together, or most assuredly we shall all hang separately!"[11]

Samuel Adams, who led the Sons of Liberty, led the Committees of Correspondence, and labored tirelessly for freedom and independence, sat silently awaiting his time to sign the sacred declaration. He was referred to as the "Lightning Rod of the American Revolution" and the "last Puritan." At the appointed time, he rose and boldly stated, "We have this day restored the Sovereign to Whom alone men ought to be obedient. He reigns in heaven and ... from the rising to the setting sun, may His kingdom come."[12]

John Adams again reflected upon the moment of freedom and the possibilities of its lasting ramifications with these statements.

> "Before God, I believe the hour has come. My judgment approves this measure, and my whole heart is in it. All that I have, and all

that I am, and all that I hope in this life, I am now ready here to stake upon it. And I leave off as I began, that live or die, survive or perish, I am for the Declaration. It is my living sentiment, and by the blessing of God it shall be my dying sentiment. Independence now, and Independence forever!

"It is the will of heaven that the two countries should be sundered forever. It may be the will of heaven that America shall suffer calamities still more wasting and distresses more dreadful. If this is to be the case, it will have this good effect, at least: it will inspire us with many virtues which we have not, and correct many errors, follies and vices, which threaten to disturb, dishonor and destroy us ... The furnace of affliction produces refinements in states, as well as individuals."[13]

25

The Hand of God

Ticonderoga

Providence, as the Christians of the eighteenth century referred to God, was continuously on the side of the untrained rabble army of the Americans. Time after time, the hand of God was obviously working to support the American cause of independence. At the Battle of Fort Ticonderoga in 1775, Colonels Ethan Allen and Benedict Arnold surprised the fort at daybreak. As Allen stormed the providentially opened gate, the sentry fired at him from point blank range, but the musket did not fire. The colonists quickly subdued the small British garrison. When Colonel Allen demanded the formal surrender from the surprised British officer, he replied, "By what authority?" Allen's bold reply was, "In the name of the great Jehovah, and the Continental Congress." The fort was captured without a shot, and the gateway to New York was opened. The most valuable prize of the fort was arms, munitions, and cannons.

Boston

The elated General Washington quickly dispatched General Henry Knox to New York to transport those valuable spoils of the victory at Ticonderoga to the eastern front at Boston. When Knox arrived at Washington's headquarters in late January with 43 cannons and 16 mortars, the continental commander took the offensive for the first time in the war. For months, Washington waited outside Boston for the British General Howe to attack him. The Americans suffered through the winter without sufficient food, clothing or even military supplies. At one point of the winter encampment, it was estimated that Washington's army had only enough gunpowder to supply each soldier with nine rounds of firepower. When this information was leaked to General Howe, he discounted the rumor as false, too unbelievable to be taken seriously.

On March 4, 1776, General Washington moved the captured artillery pieces into place at Dorchester Heights overlooking Boston. General William Howe arrogantly refused to occupy this strategic position, feeling that it would be useless to the rebels who had no cannons to use against him. On the morning of March 5, the British commander realized his mistake as the Americans labored tirelessly all night to occupy the high ground.

Howe countered Washington's move by ordering 2,200 British regulars to ferry across the harbor from Boston to seize the Heights from the rabble American forces. As the British prepared to board their boats, an unexpected storm suddenly blew in off the Atlantic. One observer called the force a "hurricane," and another stated that it "was of an intensity that few had seen."[1] Torrents of rain and unbelievable winds scattered the British ships and sent the troops packing, back to the safety of their barracks. The relentless storm lasted three days. What followed was even more amazing. Instead of continuing the invasion and attack, General Howe evacuated the city, surrendering the patriots' stronghold without a shot.

Instead of a public celebration to ridicule the retreating British and loyal Tories, Washington called for church services and a day of prayer and thanksgiving. He wrote his brother Augustine of God's action at Boston. "This most remarkable interposition of Providence is for some wise purpose I have not a doubt."[2]

Boston was liberated without the loss of a single man. The war that could have ended with just one British attack was sustained by the providence of God. General Howe not only evacuated the city, but he left weapons, gunpowder, and 250 artillery pieces for the use of the Continental Army. More importantly, the cause of liberty was still alive. Confidence in Washington, his army and the nation was growing. God had validated the Declaration of Independence four months before it was signed.

New York

In June 1776, the British fleet sailed into New York Harbor. Their plan was to amass the largest overseas land army that the British empire had ever seen. Since New York was the commercial and transportation hub that united the colonies, it was the target of British occupation. General Howe's strategy was to divide the northern and southern colonies from a strong base at New York.

General Washington realized the importance of the city, the harbor and the surrounding regions. He rushed to New York and issued this order on July 2, 1776.

> "The time is now near at hand which must probably determine whether Americans are to be freemen or slaves; whether they are to have any property they can call their own; whether their houses and farms are to be pillaged and destroyed, and themselves consigned to a state of wretchedness from which no human efforts will deliver them.
>
> "The fate of unborn millions will now depend, under God, on the courage of this army. Our cruel and unrelenting enemy leaves us only the choice of brave resistance, or the most abject submission. We have, therefore, to resolve to conquer or die."[3]

The main resistance by colonial forces was at Brooklyn on the western end of Long Island. On the morning of August 22, 1776, 20,000 British troops went ashore near Brooklyn. Washington's opposition forces amounted to 8,000 militia and continentals. In five days the Americans were hopelessly cut off and trapped by General Howe's redcoats and German mercenaries. All afternoon, after fierce morning fighting, General Washington watched from a vantage point of safety as his troops awaited capture or death. The Redcoats and German mercenaries had inflicted nearly 1,000 casualties on the noble American force, which had fallen back to its inner defenses.

And so they waited...and waited. And waited. And never knew that God was with them all the time. For Howe, against all military logic, was once again failing to follow up his all-too-obvious advantage. And this was not a dull general! His surrounding maneuver of the night before had been brilliantly conceived and flawlessly executed, taking the Americans entirely by surprise. As afternoon became evening, and the night wore on silently and peacefully, it gradually became apparent that Howe was not going to attack. Unbelievable! A miracle, a few would begin to say. Yet Howe's unaccountable delay was only the opening curtain on what would be the most amazing episode of divine intervention in the Revolutionary War.[4]

On August 29, Washington realized his precarious situation and developed a plan to move his battered, outnumbered army to safety across the East River. But the action would have to be performed flawlessly, with the utmost secrecy. All day, the American army assembled every boat possible to ferry its troops to safety. Under cover of darkness, Washington ordered his men to systematically retreat to the boats while a token force remained on the front lines to keep the appearance of an army present on the field. Even though there was no way to hold off a British attack all night, the Americans kept up the ruse. At 11:00 p.m., the wind died down, making transporting the troops across the river easier, but it became apparent that the entire force would not be evacuated before dawn. Washington himself supervised the loading, knowing that he would be captured if all did not go as planned.

All did not go well for the Americans. At midnight, the storm winds stopped and clouds parted, leaving clear moonlight, sheer death for the mini American armada. But it was as if the British were asleep. The colonials continued all night to shuttle troops, un-harassed, across the two miles of the East River. At nearly 2:00 a.m., the last troops were erroneously ordered off the lines. All fell silent along the American lines. Almost an hour passed before the brave patriots could be ordered back in place to defend against an attack and keep up the trickery.

At the same time, an English sympathizer, Mrs. John Repelye, noticed the American evacuation. She sent her servant to inform the British. This Tory carrying the message of Washington's escape would be disastrous to the American retreat if he reached the British. Upon passing the American lines, the servant was picked up by a British patrol of Hessians. Since the Germans could not speak English, they held the messenger until morning, when they finally found an English officer to hear his report.

Just before dawn, Washington and hundreds of his loyal troops seemed to be hopelessly trapped on Long Island. The American commander was committed to being the last soldier to evacuate, but there were not enough boats to ferry them under the cover of darkness. Then the unthinkable happened. Dense fog came out of nowhere. Major Benjamin Tallmadge described it thus:

> "As the dawn of the next day approached, those of us who remained in the trenches became very anxious for our own safety, and when the dawn appeared there were several regiments still on duty. At this time a very dense fog began to rise, and it seemed to settle in a peculiar manner over both encampments. I recollect this peculiar providential occurrence perfectly well; and so very dense was the atmosphere that I could scarcely discern a man at six yards distance. The providential appearance of the fog saved a part of our army from being captured, and certainly myself among others who formed the rear guard."[5]

The fog provided just enough time for Washington to withdraw his front line defenses and get everyone in the boats. He was in the last boat to shove off and drew enemy fire. The "Heavenly Messenger," as one soldier put it, enabled Washington and all but four men to escape.

> Amazingly, the entire force, at least nine thousand troops, possibly more, plus baggage, provisions, horses, field guns, everything but five heavy cannon that were too deep in the mud to budge, had been transported over the river in a single night with a makeshift emergency armada assembled in a matter of hours. Not a life was lost. It is not even known that anyone was injured.[6]

This mysterious compilation of events saved Washington's army – General Howe's cautious approach to Washington's desperate situation at Brooklyn Heights, the northeast winds that kept the British fleet from assisting in the attack on Long Island, the inexplicable fog which shrouded the American withdrawal, and the unheard message that the Americans were escaping.

Trenton

Following the embarrassing defeat at Long Island, General Washington retreated north into New York and then south through New Jersey into Pennsylvania.

In November, almost 3,000 Continental soldiers were captured when Fort Washington was surrendered to General Howe's British redcoats. To further complicate Washington's woes, nearly 2,000 of his militiamen went home the same month. By December 1, the Continental Army of Washington numbered only 3,000 poorly equipped and demoralized men. The enlistments of many of these would expire at the end of the year and most were expected to return home. Early that winter, Washington ordered colonial General Charles Lee to combine their forces in Pennsylvania. General Lee, who hoped to replace Washington as commander of all continental forces, refused to comply with Washington's order.

With his army dissolving before him and his generals conspiring to undermine him, the noble Virginian developed a daring plan to attack the Hessian garrison at Trenton, New Jersey. Washington and 2,400 men made a night crossing of the nearly frozen Delaware River on Christmas day, 1776. The weather was almost unbearably cold. Sleet and snow hampered the marching army, but concealed their movement as well. The element of surprise was essential to Washington's bold plan. Two events nearly changed the outcome of the raid. First, the Hessian troopers were alerted to the impending attack by a loyalist who lived near Trenton. The arrogant Colonel Johann Rall, who commanded the garrison, did little to prepare for the "rebel" threat. Around 7:00 p.m., firing broke out near the edge of the town. The Hessian mercenaries responded in force, which sent the small detail of unknown patriots retreating up the

Pennington Road. Once the perimeter was secure, Colonel Rall returned to his evening of cards and drinking, assuming the supposed attack was repulsed. In reality, the 7:00 p.m. skirmish had nothing to do with Washington's plan of attack. Instead of alerting the Hessians, it put them at ease.

The second near-disastrous event came later in the night, while Colonel Rall was being entertained at the Abraham Hunt home. A Tory farmer from Pennsylvania came to the Hunts to notify the smug German that Washington had crossed the Delaware and was marching on Trenton. The Colonel's servant would not allow the commanding officer to be interrupted, but did deliver a written message disclosing the impending danger. Colonel Rall placed the unread note in his coat pocket, while he continued to gamble the night away.[7]

At 8:00 a.m., Washington gave the order for his nearly frozen men to attack. The surprised Hessians fought gallantly, but casualties were high. In approximately an hour of hand-to-hand combat, the Hessian garrison was completely routed by the ill-supplied, under-nourished and undisciplined American forces. One officer claimed 100 Hessians dead, although Washington placed the number at 20 to 30. Approximately 900 prisoners were taken and several hundred more fled in horror into the freezing snow. General Washington's casualties were a handful of wounded, including his cousin, William Washington and future president, Lieutenant James Monroe. It was also reported that up to five patriots froze to death in the frigid Christmas offensive.

Three days later, the jubilant Continentals crossed back into Pennsylvania, supplied with confiscated British weapons, powder and food supplies. They also carried with them an immeasurable amount of strength that came from not only whipping a disciplined, equipped force of mercenaries, but also knowing that God had delivered them again. A survey of the battle found the surprised garrison commander, Colonel Rall, lying dead on the battlefield with the note about the planned surprise attack of the Americans still in his pocket.[8] American General Henry Knox wrote, "Providence seemed to have smiled upon every part of this enterprise."[9] The colonials ended 1776 with a smashing military victory at Trenton, which restored confidence in General Washington and his brave army.

On January 2, General Charles Cornwallis left Princeton, New Jersey, and quickly marched toward Trenton to capture Washington and defend British honor following the December 26 humiliation. He bragged to the quartermaster that he would "bag the fox"[10] the next morning. Under cover of darkness, the fox, Washington, and his men flanked the British army, marched about ten miles, and captured the reserves that Cornwallis had left at Princeton. Once again, the American army had avoided defeat and the wily Washington escaped back to the safety of Pennsylvania.

Saratoga

Following a stalemate in the summer of 1777, George Washington's Continentals were miserably defeated on September 11 at Brandywine, and the Continental Congress was forced to flee Philadelphia. In October, Washington's forces were again defeated at the Battle of Germantown. Patriotism was waning and morale was low. The capital was an occupied city, the American commander-in-chief was in retreat, and loyalists were clamoring for a cessation to the war. Americans needed a decisive military victory, and they desperately needed help from abroad. By the end of the year, they would have both, along with the divine intervention of Heaven.

In the fall of 1777, the American forces, under General Horatio Gates, managed to not only contain the British forces under General John Burgoyne, but actually forced the surrender of over 5,000 men and a cache of military supplies at Saratoga, New York. Burgoyne's grand campaign actually began on June 13 with a force of 7,000 trained "regulars" and mercenaries. It ended in total disaster after defeats at Bennington, and Fireman's Farm.

> The Providence of God was evident in this victory. Earlier, General Howe was supposed to have marched north to join Burgoyne's 11,000 men at Saratoga. However, in his haste to leave London for a holiday, Lord North forgot to sign the dispatch to General Howe. The dispatch was pigeonholed and not

found until years later in the archives of the British army. This inadvertence, plus the fact that contrary winds kept British reinforcements delayed at sea for three months, totally altered the outcome at Saratoga in favor of America.[11]

Upon hearing of the great victory, the Continental Congress made a National Proclamation of Thanksgiving, as stated below:

"Forasmuch as it is the indispensable duty of all men to adore the superintending Providence of Almighty God; to acknowledge with gratitude their obligation to Him for benefits received and to implore such further blessing as they stand in need of; and it having pleased Him in His abundant mercy not only to continue to us the innumerable bounties of His common Providence... to smile upon us as in the prosecution of a just and necessary war for the defense and establishment of our unalienable rights and liberties..."[12]

Many military historians believe that the American victory at Saratoga was the turning point of the War of Independence. By the dawn of 1778, the British threat in the North was all but eliminated. George Washington could, for the first time, fight a "one front" war. The American forces of the North could be transferred to Washington's direct command in Pennsylvania. Guarding the Canadian border from

British attack would be the responsibility of local militia, while Washington could address the main threat of General Howe's army at New York City.

In December, when the French King Louis XVI learned of the impressive American victory at Saratoga, he committed the aid of his country to Benjamin Franklin, the American ambassador in Paris. Without the aid of the French, most historians feel that America would not have gained her independence from Great Britain.

Valley Forge

The Valley Forge experience of 1777-1778 defined the American struggle for independence. Washington's troops were besieged on every side, but not by enemy forces. Valley Forge was not a battle; it was a cruel winter's encampment. The loyal Continental Army struggled against the elements: a long cold winter, political bickering from Congress, and horrible sickness. One in four died. It was at this point that Washington rose to greatness. Providence led him to Valley Forge, Pennsylvania. There he found ample water, forest for cabins, and enough distance from the British army to survive. The winter was costly, long and bitter. Washington wrote of the experience.

> "No history now extant can furnish an instance of an army's suffering such uncommon hardships as ours has done and bearing them with

the same patience and fortitude. To see men without clothes to cover their nakedness, without blankets to lie on, without shoes (for the want of which their marches might be traced by the blood of their feet)...and submitting without a murmur is a proof of patience and obedience which in my opinion can scarce be paralleled."[13]

It was at Valley Forge that Washington's troops learned toughness, discipline and faith. It was the faith and example of their beloved general that sustained them in those dark times. Henry Muhlenberg, a local Lutheran pastor, writes of Washington:

"I heard a fine example today, namely, that His Excellency General Washington rode around among his army yesterday and admonished each and every one to fear God, to put away his wickedness that has set in and become so general, and to practice the Christian virtues. From all appearances, this gentleman does not belong to the so-called world of society, for he respects God's Word, believes in the atonement through Christ, and bears himself in humility and gentleness. Therefore, the Lord God has also singularly, yea, marvelously, preserved him from harm in the midst of countless perils, ambuscades, fatigues, etc., and has hitherto graciously held him in His hand as a chosen vessel."[14]

As General George Washington was the spiritual and moral force for the Continental Army at Valley Forge, Baron von Stueben became its disciplinarian.

> The soldiers who came through Valley Forge were tempered into the carbon-steel core around which an army could be built. In the tempering process, God sent...a ruddy-cheeked bemedaled German with a passion for drill, and a twinkle in his eye. This was Friedrich Wilhelm Augustus Baron von Stueben, a former captain in the Prussian army and staff officer of Frederick the Great. Well recommended by Ben Franklin in Paris, von Stueben volunteered his services to the American cause. Washington quickly recognized his expertise, and assigned him the task of making a professional army out of the Continentals.[15]

The spring of 1778 brought new hope for colonials. The French were committing their aid to the "American Cause." Washington's forces held out through the bitter winter to find enlistments high with the news of France's intervention into the war. The jubilant continental commander announced to his army:

> "It having pleased the Almighty Ruler of the universe to defend the cause of the United American States, and finally to raise up a powerful friend among the princes of the

earth, to establish our liberty and independence upon a lasting foundation, it becomes us to set apart a day for gratefully acknowledging the divine goodness, and celebrating the important event, which we owe to His divine interposition."[16]

Monmouth

In June of 1778, the American army left Valley Forge a transformed army. Washington boldly took the offensive at Monmouth, New Jersey, against a new British commander, General Henry Clinton. Though outnumbered, Washington was not out manned. The Americans held the field following the battle and sent the British retreating back to New York, having lost one-fifth of their force.

Following the disastrous campaign of 1777, which climaxed with the loss of an entire army, the British ministry in London developed a new plan to retain their colonial empire in America. General Clinton would concentrate on victory in the southern colonies. Since the main resistance had been in New England, the British hoped to divide the colonies, and if a peace treaty was signed short of complete surrender by the colonies, the mother country hoped to retain at least the southern states.

The winter of 1777-78 had been the darkest for the American cause. Washington had lost nearly one-fourth of his army without engaging the enemy or firing a shot at Valley Forge. If the British had successfully reinforced General Burgoyne in the North, General Gates would have been defeated in New York. But God granted grace to Washington and victory to Gates, and by mid 1778, the complexion of war in America was totally different. By the second anniversary of the Declaration of Independence, the British had sent a peace commission to Philadelphia to talk of ending the war. Their offers were rejected by the Continental Congress who, encouraged by the French alliance, insisted on complete independence. How could they negotiate? The blood of brave American patriots cried out for freedom from tyranny instead of peace at any price.

In July of 1778, the long-awaited French fleet reached America. Colonial hopes were once again renewed. However, in September, Benjamin Lincoln suffered a miserable defeat at Savannah, Georgia. By the end of the year, events would be totally different.

> At Cowpens, South Carolina, on January 17, 1781, [General George] Morgan again displayed his exceptional military skill by executing the most nearly perfect victory of the war. The Americans feigned a retreat and then dramatically halted and repelled the reckless British pursuit. Morgan's skill as a commander helped cause the British to retreat in panic. The British suffered 930 casualties, the Americans only 70. The Battle of Cowpens was the first major step toward eventual British defeat.[17]

Charles Cornwallis, the British Commander of the southern theater, was infuriated at the miserable defeat of Colonel Banastre Tarleton at the Battle of Cowpens. He vowed a quick revenge. Destroying his own baggage wagons, he quickly moved south to cut off Morgan's advance into North Carolina. Cornwallis, confident of smashing the American force, failed to cross the Catawba River to engage Morgan. The night before the grand British attack of reprisal, a storm filled the river, making it impossible to cross. Morgan's army retreated to safety. Twice more the angry British general nearly caught the illusive Morgan, but both times the American slipped sway. On February 3, another providential flood protected the American forces. Ten days later, Morgan's army was saved by yet another "act of God," with a winter flood. The British were amazed at the miraculous acts. "Even Clinton, the commander-in-chief of Lord Cornwallis, acknowledged that Divine Providence had intervened."[18]

West Point

The Battle of West Point was the battle that never was. For years following the successful American campaign, which climaxed with the glorious victory at Saratoga, General Benedict Arnold had been consumed with envy and hatred over General Horatio Gates' failure to acknowledge his contribution at Saratoga. Gates omitted mention of Arnold's contribution during battle. This tragic omission caused an open wound between the two American generals. Arnold obviously felt that he deserved more credit for the success of the campaign and the ultimate victory at Saratoga. By 1780, Arnold had his own command at West Point, New York, but for months he had secretly been giving British commander Henry Clinton information about Washington's movements. In the fall of 1780, he was conspiring to surrender his forces at West Point to the British. Only an act of God would prevent such a treacherous act.

On September 23, three young patriots, volunteer military men, posted themselves outside Tarrytown, New York. They hoped to stop Tory "cowboys" from stealing cattle from American farmers in the area and providing them to the enemy for beef. By chance, they stopped what they believed to be a civilian headed toward British-occupied New York City. It was revealed after a search that the detainee was, in reality, a British officer in civilian clothing. Major John Andrea had papers on him from Benedict Arnold, incriminating the American general of treason. Andrea attempted to bribe the young soldiers, but was turned over to American authorities. He was tried for being a spy and executed. Arnold, on the other hand, escaped to British safety, but his garrison was saved. General Washington wrote to John Laurens of the treachery of Arnold and the divine intervention of God.

> "In no instance since the commencement of the War has the interposition of Providence appeared more conspicuous than in the rescue of the Post and Garrison of West Point from

Arnold's villainous perfidy...A combination of extraordinary circumstances."[19]

General Washington issued these orders on September 26, 1780, from his headquarters following the discovery of the incident:

"Treason of the blackest dye was yesterday discovered! General Arnold who commanded at West Point, lost to every sentiment of honor, of public and private obligation, was about to deliver up that important Post into the hands of the enemy. Such an event must have given the American cause a deadly wound if not a fatal stab. Happily the treason has been timely discovered to prevent the fatal misfortune. The Providential train of circumstances which led to it affords the most convincing proof that the liberties of America are the object of Divine Protection."[20]

Congress, in response to the providential act of preserving Arnold's army at West Point, proclaimed a day of thanksgiving and prayer for December 7, 1780.

26

The World Turned Upside Down

By April 1781, General Charles Cornwallis had been driven out of the Carolinas. He took his tired, battle-worn troops to safety on a peninsula in southeastern Virginia. Here, between the York and James Rivers, Lord Cornwallis waited for the British fleet to ferry them to safety in New York. This proved to be a mistake. Marshall and Manuel, in *The Light and the Glory*, comment on the move of Cornwallis, "The biggest mistake of all was a compound one – an accumulation of misjudgments, human errors, and the handiwork of God which wound up with Cornwallis and 6,000 British troops bottled up in Yorktown."[1]

These three acts were repeated time and time again during the War of Independence. But they were most evident at Yorktown in 1781. Washington never had the advantage of superior numbers during the war, but on the peninsula it was different. His combined French and American forces outnumbered the retreating British invaders better than two to one. Therefore, Cornwallis sadly erred in allowing himself to be trapped at Yorktown. The second error was on the part of the British Admiral Samuel Graves. Graves was to evacuate the British troops from Washington's grasp on the Virginia peninsula, but he continued the same failed British plan of slow, timid action. Graves delayed his departure from New York and arrived at the Chesapeake Bay to rescue Cornwallis one day late! The French fleet under Admiral de Grasse had already blockaded the James-York river harbors. The British ground troops were trapped between Washington's troops and the water. The British naval troop could not reach them without engaging the French fleet.

As the French ships sailed out to meet the British fleet, Admiral Graves failed to press an advantage and allowed the French to form a battle line. This enormous error of judgment could very well have cost the British Cornwallis's army and possibly the war. During the battle, the British appeared to be confused. As a result, they were outmaneuvered and were forced to retreat to New York to refit. This sealed the fate of General Cornwallis.

General Washington continued to mercilessly siege the British fortifications at Yorktown. On October 14, French and colonists stormed outlying redoubts (fortifications), capturing them in only a matter of minutes. Cornwallis's only escape was to ferry his men across the York River under cover of night. This was a daring plan, one that Washington had successfully attempted four year earlier at Brooklyn Heights.

On October 16, in the darkness of the night, Cornwallis began this small boat evacuation across the York River. He succeeded in getting a third of his force across before a storm stopped their progress.

A sudden violent storm of wind and rain came up out of nowhere, driving the boats down river and making further passage impossible. By the time the storm subsided, too many hours had been lost to complete the evacuation, so Cornwallis ordered the troops on the far side of the river to be brought back. As the last boats returned at daybreak, they came under the heaviest American artillery fire yet. As General Banistre Tarleton said, 'Thus expired the last hope of the British Army.'[2]

Once again, the forces of man had to succumb to the powerful hand of God. The British were hopelessly trapped. The next morning, American artillery began a fresh bombardment of the town. Before noon, Cornwallis had raised a flag of truce. The formal surrender was set for 2:00 p.m. the next day. The seasoned colonial officers of Washington's command all marveled that the arrogant Cornwallis gave up so abruptly, almost without a fight. Though Lord Cornwallis pled ill, his subordinates surrendered his entire command of 6,000 to the combined forces of Washington and Rochambeau. With the British band playing, General Charles O'Hara rode at the head of the surrender party to formally present his sword to the allied victors. The defeated general attempted to surrender to French General Rochambeau, who refused the insult which was obviously aimed at Washington. The French count politely directed O'Hara to the Commander of the Continental Armies, George Washington. The American general instructed his second in command, General Benjamin Lincoln, to receive the surrender.[3] Ironically, it was Lincoln who just a year before suffered America's greatest defeat of the war, as he surrendered his sword to General Clinton at Savannah. Earlier, Cornwallis had boasted that he would bag the fox (Washington).[4] The fox had not only eluded Cornwallis at Princeton in 1778, but now the wily American general had captured the brash British general and would send him back to England in disgrace.

As the British red-coated regulars paraded to the surrender field to stack arms, the royal musicians played the popular tune of the day, "The World Turned Upside Down." What a harbinger of the future. The most powerful army on the face of the earth was surrendering to a rag-tag militia of rebels. General Washington ordered a thanksgiving service on the day after the surrender. His order stated, "The Commander-in-Chief earnestly recommends that the troops not on duty should universally attend with that seriousness of deportment and gratitude of heart which the recognition of such reiterated and astonishing interposition of Providence demands of us."[5] The American Commander-in-Chief related his inner feelings of gratitude to God by stating, "The hand of Providence has been so conspicuous in all this, that he must be worse than an infidel that lacks faith, and more than wicked, that has not gratitude enough to acknowledge his obligation."[6] His official report to the president of Congress stated, "I take a particular pleasure in acknowledging that the interposing Hand of Heaven, in the various instances of our extensive Preparation for this Operation [Yorktown], has been most conspicuous and remarkable."[7]

All across the colonies, church bells tolled. Thanks was given and sermons preached, for God's hand was truly upon America. Timothy Dewight, the patriot and president of Yale University, in his sermon on thanksgiving following the British surrender of Yorktown, said the following:

> "Who, but must remember with hymns of the most fervent praise, how God judged our enemies, when we had no might against the great company that came against us, neither knew we what to do? But our eyes were upon Him. Who, but must give glory to the infinite Name, when he calls to mind that our most important successes, in almost every instance have happened when we were peculiarly weak and distressed? While we mark the Divine hand in the illustrious event we are now contemplating, can we fail to cry out, "Praise the Lord, for He is good, for His mercy endureth forever."[8]

When England's Prime Minister, Lord North, heard of Yorktown, he replied, "It's all over," and promptly resigned, and King George III went so far as to draft a message of abdication. But in reality, it was not over. Scattered fighting continued for another year. Vicious battles were fought between Loyalists and Patriots, especially on the frontier. A Delaware Indian village in the Ohio Valley was massacred by a band of American militia. The event was tragic in that many of the inhabitants were devout Christians and innocent of the terrorism of the Indians and the massacre. A lesser-known tragedy is commemorated by the Martyr's Tomb in New York. This memorial was erected to the nearly 11,000 soldiers and civilians who perished in the holds of British prisoner ships during the war.

On September 3, 1783, after months of negotiation, the Treaty of Paris was finally signed. The treaty formally ended the war. It acknowledged that the colonies were free and independent. America was awarded all the land east of the Mississippi River, with the exception of Florida, which returned to Spanish control. Britain also guaranteed her the use of the Mississippi for trade, despite the fact that Spain, not Britain, controlled the entrance to the Mississippi at New Orleans.

The war was over. The colonies were finally free. Soldiers could go home to continue their lives as private citizens, and statesman could build a nation. In 1783, Washington resigned his commission as Commander-in-chief in the following way.

> "I consider it an indispensable duty to close this last solemn act of my official life by commending the interests of our dearest

country to the protection of Almighty God, and of those who have superintendence of them to His holy keeping ... Having now finished the work assigned me, I retire from the great theatre of action, and bidding affectionate farewell to the august body under whose orders I have so long acted, I here offer my commission and take my leave of all the employments of public life."[9]

With this great address, Washington retreated to Mount Vernon to leave public life and allow others to govern the infant nation. He must have pondered what would become of this country for which he and other brave patriots had fought and thousands had died.

By 1783, all the states had adopted the Articles of Confederation and a national union existed. But the loose confederation of states so feared the centralization of power that the federal government could not function. It had no power to raise revenue, no real authority to enforce its own legislation, and no executive to lead. For over a decade, the fledgling nation struggled for existence. A mere confederation of states could not survive without more centralized power, an improved federal structure, and a capable leader. In 1787, the Constitution was drafted, providing both central authority and a federal structure for government. Two years later, enough states ratified the new form of government and the Constitution replaced the Articles of Confederation. On April 6, 1789, George Washington was elected the first President.

The United States of America was truly a nation. Through the epic struggle of the War of Independence, the states shook off the suppressive yoke of English bondage and emerged as a separate and free nation. Truly, the world had turned upside down. With the dawning of a new nation in 1789, President Washington could only dream as to the success or failure of his infant republic. Washington and the founders did dream of a country that would become strong and endure long as one nation under God.

Note to the Reader:

Since history is "His Story," no study of America's founding can be fully understood outside of a personal relationship with our Creator.

God longs for the restored relationships with man that sin robs us of. By accepting Christ as our savior, that relationship with God is restored.

The scriptures provide us all directions for the path back to God. We must:

1. Realize that We are Sinners.

Everyone starts at the same place spiritually in their walk with God. We are all sinners. Romans 3:23 states: "For all have sinned and come short of the glory of God."

2. Realize there is a Penalty for Sin.

Not only does our sin keep us from Heaven, but it also condemns us to Hell. Romans 6:23 says, "For the wages of sin is death."

3. Realize Jesus Paid our Debt.

Christ took our place, and died for us so we can be saved. Romans 5:8 illustrates our Lord's love for us. "But God commendeth his love toward us, in that while we were yet sinners, Christ died for us."

4. Repent of our Sins and Receive Christ as our Savior.

Repentance means to turn from our sins and follow Christ. Romans 10:9 states: "That if thou shalt confess with thy mouth the Lord Jesus and shalt believe in thine heart that God hath raised him from the dead, thou shalt be saved."

Once a person receives Christ, his relationship is restored with God and his walk of faith begins. If you need help in your walk with God, please contact us at the ministry address below. Thank you for reading ***Dawn's Early Light***. God bless you as you walk in His light.

Larry Haggard

Cross Roads Ministries
919 Gum Branch Rd.
Jacksonville, NC 28540

jcapastor@ec.rr.com

ENDNOTES

Chapter 1 - The Early Light

1. Glen Chambers and Gene Fisher, *United States History for Christian Schools*, (Greenville, SC: Bob Jones University Press, 1982), p. 16.

Chapter 2 - The Christ Bearer

1. Washington Irving, *The Life and Voyages of Christopher Columbus,* (New York: PF Collier and Son, 1868), Vol. I, p. 37.
2. Ibid., p. 69.
3. Ibid., p. 164.
4. Ibid., p. 126-127.
5. Peter Marshall and David Manuel, *The Light and the Glory*, (Grand Rapids, MI: Fleming H. Revell, 1977), p. 35.
6. Irving, p. 139.
7. Marshall and Manuel, p. 41.
8. Ibid., p. 41.
9. Ibid., p. 52.
10. Irving, p. 331.

11. Zvi Dor-Ner, ***Columbus and the Age of Discovery,*** (New York: William Morrow Co., 1991), p. 119. (Note: Converted to US dollars by using the GNP table)
12. Chambers and Fisher, p. 25.
13. Ibid., p. 25.
14. J. Steven Wilkins, ***America, the First 350 Years,*** (Forest, MS: Covenant Publishing, 1988), p. 4.
15. Marshall and Manuel, p. 66.

Chapter 3 - God or Gold

1. Chambers and Fisher, p. 29.
2. Arthur Schlesinger, Jr., ed., ***The Almanac of American History,*** (New York: Perigee Books, 1983), p. 26.
3. Marshall and Manuel, p. 59.

Chapter 4 - A Consuming Fire

1. Laurel Hicks, ed., ***The Modern Age,*** (Pensacola, FL: A-Beka Book Publishing, 1981), p. 22.
2. Ibid., p. 30.
3. Ibid., p. 41.
4. Ken Connolly, ***The Church in Transition,*** (Shreveport, LA: Lin Vel Books, 1984), p. 41.

Chapter 5 - The Protestant Wind

1. Hicks, p. 153.
2. Ibid., p. 154.

3. Felipe Fernandez - Armesto, ***The Spanish Armada,*** (Oxford: Oxford University Press, 1988), p. 37.
4. Ibid., p. 38.
5. Ibid., p. 34.
6. Ibid., p. 41-42.
7. Ibid., p. 197.
8. Ibid., p. 40.
9. Ibid., p. 238.
10. Ibid., p. 238.
11. Ibid., p. 43.

Chapter 6 - The Forbidden Book

1. Connolly, p, 73.
2. Mark A. Beliles and Stephen K. McDowell, ***America's Providential History,*** (Charlottesville, VA: Providence Foundation, 1989), p. 53.
3. Craig Lampe, ***The Forbidden Book,*** (Phoenix, AZ, 2003), p. 57.
4. Beliles and McDowell, p. 54.
5. Ibid., p. 54.
6. Benson Bobrick, ***Wide as the Waters, the Story of the English Bible and the Revolution it Inspired,*** (New York: Penguin Books, 2001), p. 164.
7. Beliles and McDowell, p. 56-57.
8. Bobrick, p. 186.
9. Lampe, p. 74-75.

Chapter 7 - God Has a Plan

1. Ronald A. Horton, *British Literature,* (Pensacola, FL: A-Beka Book Publishing, 1993), p. 71.
2. Don Boys, *Pilgrims, Puritans and Patriots, Our Christian Heritage,* (Indianapolis: Good Hope Press, 1985), p. 55-56.
3. Gary DeMar, *America's Christian Heritage: The Untold Story,* (Atlanta: American Vision, Inc., 1993), p. 52.
4. Charles Thompson, *The Religious Foundations of America: A Study in National Origins,* (New York: Fleming H. Revell, 1917), p. 81.
5. Paul S. Newman, *In God We Trust: America's Heritage of Faith,* (Norwalk, CT: C.R. Gibson and Co., 1974), p. 24.
6. Boys, p. 63.
7. Ibid., p. 63.
8. Ibid., p. 64.
9. Ibid., p. 65-66.
10. DeMar, p. 53.
11. Chambers and Fisher, p. 37.
12. B. F. Morris, *The Christian Life and Character of Civil Institutions of the United States,* (Philadelphia: George N. Childs Publishing, 1864), p. 94.

Chapter 8 - In the Name of God - Amen

1. Barton W. Folsom, Jr., *The Spirit of Freedom: Essays in American History,* (Irving-on-Hudson,

NY: The Foundation for Economic Education, Inc., 1994), p. 8.
2. William Bradford, *Of Plymouth Plantation 1620-1647,* (New York: Alfred A. Knopf Co., 1952), p. 17-18.
3. Ibid., p. 23-24.
4. Ibid., p. 24.
5. Ibid., p. 25.
6. Ibid., p. 26.
7. Folsom, p. 7.
8. Bradford, p. 31.
9. Ibid., p. 31-32.
10. Ibid., p. 32-33.
11. Ibid., p. 41.
12. Ibid., p. 58.
13. Ibid., p. 60.
14. Ibid., p. 66.
15. Mortimer Adler, Editor in Chief, *The Annals of America,* (Chicago: Encyclopedia Britannica, Inc., 1976), Vol. I, p. 64.
16. Ibid., p. 64.
17. Bradford, p. 80-81.
18. Marshall and Manuel, p. 132.
19. Wilkins, p. 9.
20. Ibid., p. 9.
21. Marshall and Manuel, p. 141.
22. Bradford, p. 171.

Chapter 9 - A City Upon a Hill

1. Wilkins, p. 11.
2. Marshall and Manuel, p. 155.

3. E. S. Gausted, ed., *A Documentary History of Religion in America to the Civil War,* (Grand Rapids: Erdmands, 1985), p. 104-105.
4. Boys, p. 137-138.
5. Marshall and Manuel, p. 161.
6. Ibid., p. 162.
7. Gregg C. Singer, *The Theological Interpretation of American History,* (Phillipsburg, NJ: Presbyterian and Reformed Publishing, 1964), p. 14.
8. Ibid., p. 16.

Chapter 10 - Conceived in Liberty

1. Wilkins, p. 11.
2. Adler, Vol. I, p. 167.
3. David C. Gibbs, Jr., *One Nation Under God: Ten Things Every Christian Should Know About the Founding of America,* (Seminole, FL: Christian Law Association, 2003), p. 38.
4. Ibid., p. 42.
5. Verna Hall, ed., *The Christian History of the Constitution of the United States of America,* (San Francisco: Foundation for American Christian Education, 1993), p. 252.
6. Gibbs, p. 46.

Chapter 11 - The Most Misunderstood Man in America

1. Timothy Hall, *Separating Church and State, Roger Williams and Religious Liberty,* (Urbana: University-of Illinois, 1998), p. 18.

2. Marshall and Manuel, p. 193.
3. Timothy Hall, p. 38-39.
4. Ibid., p. 39.
5. Boys, p. 181-182.
6. Wilkins, p. 24.
7. Marshall and Manuel, p. 192-193.
8. Richard B. Cook, *The Story of the Baptists,* (Baltimore: R. H. Woodward Co., 1891), p. 201.
9. William P. Grady, *What Hath God Wrought,* (Schererville, IN: Grady Publications, 1996), p. 77.
10. Wilkins, p. 24.
11. Timothy Hall, p. 26.
12. Marshall and Manuel, p. 197.
13. Timothy Hall, p. 27.

Chapter 12 - The Rise of Other Colonies in America

1. Adler, Vol. I, p. 88.
2. Morris, p. 94.
3. Adler, Vol. I, p. 263.
4. DeMar, p. 59.
5. Ibid., p. 59.
6. Adler, Vol. I, p. 88-89.
7. Chambers and Fisher, p. 43.
8. Murray Rothbard, *Conceived in Liberty,* (New Rochelle, NY: Arlington House Publishers, 1975), Vol. I, p. 197.
9. Ibid., Vol. I, p. 125.
10. DeMar, p. 77.

11. Gibbs, p. 58.
12. Rothbard, Vol. II, p. 111.

Chapter 13 - The Salem Witch Trials

1. Wilkins, p. 31.
2. Ibid., p. 31.
3. Ibid., p. 29.

Chapter 14 - Missions in America

1. Marshall and Manuel, p. 104-105.
2. George Bancroft, *History of the United States of America from the Discovery of the Continent,* (New York: D. Appleton and Company, 1859/1890), Vol. I, p. 228.
3. Chambers and Fisher, p. 79.

Chapter 15 - In Adam's Fall, We Sinned All

1. Chambers and Fisher, p. 61-62.
2. Adler, Vol. I, p. 170.
3. Ibid., Vol. I, p. 184.
4. Gibbs, p. 66.
5. *The New England Primer,* (Boston: Edward Drapers Printing Office, 1690/1777, Reprinted by David Barton, Wallbuilders, Aledo, TX, 1991), p. 10.
6. DeMar, p. 109.
7. Adler, Vol. I, p. 175.
8. Gibbs, p. 70.
9. Adler, Vol. I, p. 176-177.

10. DeMar, p. 105.
11. Adler, Vol. I, p. 369-372.
12. Gibbs, p. 76.

Chapter 16 - Wars and Rumors of War

1. Marshall and Manuel, p. 233.
2. Ibid., p. 233.
3. James McPherson and Alan Brinkley, General Editors, ***Days of Destiny,*** (London: DK Publishing, 2001), p. 23-24.

Chapter 17 - Pilgrim's Progress

1. Clarence Carson, ***A Basic History of the United States,*** (Wadley, AL: American Textbook Committee, 1983), Vol. I, p. 85.
2. Ibid., p. 85.
3. Benjamin Hart, ***Faith and Freedom,*** (Dallas: Lewis and Stanley Publishing, 1988), p. 171.
4. Ibid., p. 171.
5. Ibid., p. 172.
6. Ibid., p. 182.
7. Chambers and Fisher, p. 69.
8. Boys, p. 215.
9. Edward T. Hiscox, ***The New Directory for Baptist Churches,*** (Chicago: Judson Press, 1894), p. 509-510.
10. Grady, p. 110. :
11. Hiscox, p. 514.
12. Grady, p. 111.

Chapter 18 - A Sleeping Giant

1. Chambers and Fisher, p. 81.
2. Grady, p. 88.
3. DeMar, p. 104-105.

Chapter 19 - The Great Awakening

1. Marshall and Manuel, p. 241.
2. Keith J. Hardman, *Seasons of Refreshing,* (Grand Rapids: Baker Books, 1994), p. 61.
3. Carson, p. 100.
4. Hardman, p. 65.
5. Ibid., p. 67.
6. Ibid., p. 89.
7. Grady, p. 101.
8. Hardman, p. 92.
9. Marshall and Manuel, p. 253.
10. Grady, p. 102-103.
11. Wilkins, p. 46.
12. Marshall and Manuel, p. 251-252.

Chapter 20 - The War to Begin All Wars -

1. Hart, p. 231.
2. Marshall Foster, *The American Covenant,* (Thousand Oaks, CA: The Mayflower Institute, Video, 1993).
3. Chambers and Fisher, p. 99.

Chapter 21 - The Battle Cry of Freedom

1. Wilkins, p. 41.
2. Ibid., p. 44.
3. Ibid., p. 46.
4. Ibid., p. 47.
5. Adler, Vol. I, p. 337-340.
6. Rousas J. Rushdooney, *American History to 1865,* Audio Cassette Series, Cassette 4.
7. Chambers and Fisher, p. 115.
8. Wilkins, p. 44.

Chapter 22 - The Shot Heard Around the World

1. Schlesinger, p. 115.
2. Ibid., p. 117.
3. Gibbs, p. 107.
4. Ibid., p. 107.
5. Marshall and Manuel, p. 274.
6. Gibbs, p. 111.
7. Ibid., p. 112.
8. William Federer, *America's God and Country Encyclopedia of Quotations,* (Coppell, TX: Fame Publishing, 1994), p. 638.

Chapter 23 - No King But King Jesus

1. Marshall and Manuel, p. 260.
2. Ibid., p. 258.
3. Ibid., p. 264.
4. Ibid., p. 264.
5. Gibbs, p. 102.

6. Ibid., p. 103-104.
7. Ibid., p. 99.

Chapter 24 - In the Course of Human Events

1. Gibbs, p. 123-124.
2. B. J. Lossing, *Signers of the Declaration of Independence,* (New York: George F. ' Cooledge and Brother, 1848, Reprinted by Wallbuilders Press, 1995), p. 244.
3. Ibid., p. 250.
4. Ibid., p. 251-252.
5. Ibid., p. 246.
6. Beliles and McDowell, p. 149.
7. Federer, p. 5.
8. Lossing, p. 247-248.
9. Federer, p. 8.
10. Beliles and McDowell, p. 148.
11. Ibid., p. 148.
12. Ibid., p. 148.
13. Federer, p. 8-9.

Chapter 25 - The Hand of God

1. Larkin Spivey, *Miracles of the American Revolution,* (Fairfax, VA: Allegiance Press, 2004), p. 128.
2. Chambers and Fisher, p. 123.
3. Federer, p. 639.
4. Marshall and Manuel, p. 313.
5. Spivey, p. 147-148.

6. Robert Crowley, ed., *What Ifs of American History,* (New York: G. P. Putnam's Sons, 2003), p. 53.
7. David McCullough, *1776,* (New York: Simon and Schuster, 2005), p. 279.
8. W. J. Wood, *Battles of the Revolutionary War 1775-1781,* (Chapel Hill, NC: Algonquin Books, 1990), p. 66.
9. Marshall and Manuel, p. 318.
10. Ibid., p. 318.
11. Beliles and McDowell, p. 162.
12. Federer, p. 147.
13. Ibid., p. 640.
14. Ibid., p. 459-460.
15. Marshall and Manuel, p. 325.
16. Federer, p. 643.
17. Chambers and Fisher, p. 137.
18. Beliles and McDowell, p. 166. :
19. Ibid., p. 163-164. :
20. Federer, p. 645.

Chapter 26 - The World Turned Upside Down

1. Marshall and Manuel, p. 329-330.
2. Ibid., p. 330-331.
3. Victor Brooks and Robert Hohwald, *How America Fought Its Wars,* (Conshohocken, PA: Combined Publishing, 1999), p. 143.
4. Ibid., p. 318.
5. Federer, p. 646.
6. Marshall and Manuel, p. 332.
7. Federer, p. 646.

8. Marshall and Manuel, p. 333.
9. Samuel Eliot Morison, *The Growth of the American Republic,* (New York: Oxford University Press, 1950), Vol. I, p. 224.
10. Marshall and Manuel, p. 335.

BIBLIOGRAPHY

Adler, Mortimer. ***The Annals of America.*** Chicago: Encyclopedia Britannica, Inc., Vol. 1-18, 1976.

Angle, Paul. ***The American Reader.*** New York: Rand McNally, 1958.

Armesto, Felipe Fernandez. ***The Spanish Armada.*** Oxford: Oxford University Press, 1988.

Barton, David. ***Original Intent, the Courts, the Constitution and Religion.*** Aledo, TX: Wallbuilders, 2000.

Bastiat, Frederick. ***The Law.*** Irvington-on-Hudson, NY: The Foundation for Economic Education, 1950.

Beer, Samuel. ***To Make a Nation.*** Cambridge, MA: The Belknap Press, 1993.

Beliles, Mark A. and Stephen K. McDowell. *America's Providential History.* Charlottesville, VA: The Providence Foundation, 1989.

Bobrick, Benson. *Wide as the Waters, the Story of the English Bible and the Revolution it Inspired.* New York: Penguin Books, 2001.

Boys, Don. *Pilgrims, Puritans, and Patriots, Our Christian Heritage.* Indianapolis: Good Hope Press, 1983.

Bradford, E. *A Worthy Company.* Westchester, IL: Crossway Books, 1982.

Bradford, William. *Of Plymouth Plantation 1620-1647.* New York: Alfred A. Knopf Co., 1952.

Brooks, Victor and Robert Hohwald. *How America Fought Its Wars.* Conshohocken, PA: Combined Publishing, 1999.

Carson, Clarence B. *A Basic History of the United States.* Wadley, AL: American Textbook Committee, 1983.

Castle, Tony. *Lives of Famous Christians.* Ann Arbor, MI: Servant Books, 1988.

Chambers, Greg and Gene Fisher. *United States History for Christian Schools.* Greenville, SC: Bob Jones University Press, 1982.

Cohen, J. M. *The Four Voyages of Christopher Columbus.* Baltimore: Penguin Books Ltd., 1969.

Combee, Jerry and Clara Hall. *Designed for Destiny.* Wheaton, IL: Tyndale House, 1985.

Connolly, Ken. *The Church in Transition.* Shreveport, LA: Lin Wel, 1984.

Cook, Richard. *The Story of the Baptists.* Baltimore: R. H. Woodward Co., 1891.

Cowley, Robert, editor. *What Ifs of American History.* New York: G. P. Putnam's Sons, 2003.

DeMar, Gary. *America's Christian History, the Untold Story.* Atlanta: American Vision, 1993.

DeMar, Gary. *God and Government, a Biblical and Historical Study,* Vol. 1-3. Atlanta: American Vision, 1989.

DeMoss, Nancy Leigh. *The Rebirth of America.* (No city given) Arthur S. DeMoss - Foundation, 1986.

Dor-Ner, Zvi. *Columbus and the Age of Discovery.* New York: William Morrow Company, 1991.

Federer, William J. ***America, God and Country Encyclopedia of Quotations.*** Coppell, TX: Fame Publishing, 1994.

Folsom, Barton W., Jr. ***The Spirit of Freedom, Essays in American History.*** Irvington-on-Hudson, NY: The Foundation for Economic Education, 1994.

Foster, Marshall and Mary Elaine Swanson. ***The American Covenant.*** Thousand Oaks, CA: The Mayflower Institute, 1992.

Foxe, John. ***Foxes Book of Martyrs.*** New Kensington, PA: Whitaker House, 1981 Abridged.

Gallivan, C. E. ***A Nation Under God.*** Waco, TX: Word Books, 1976.

Gausted, E. S., editor. ***A Documentary History of Religion in America to the Civil War.*** Grand Rapids: Erdmands, 1985.

Gibbs, David, Jr. ***One Nation Under God, Ten Things Every Christian Should Know About the Founding of America.*** Seminole, FL: Christian Law Association, 2003.

Grady, William P. ***What Hath God Wrought.*** Schererville, IN: Grady Publications, 1996.

Grant, George. ***The Patriots' Handbook.*** Elkton, MD: Highland Books, 1996.

Greeley, Horace. ***The American-Conflict, Vol. 1-2.*** Hartford: Case and Company, 1866.

Hall, Timothy. ***Separating Church and State, Roger Williams and Religious Liberty.*** Urbana, IL: University of Illinois Press, 1998.

Hall, Verna and Rosalie Slater. ***The Bible and the Constitution of the United States of America.*** San Francisco: Foundation for American Christian Education, 1983.

Hardman, Keith J. ***Seasons of Refreshing.*** Grand Rapids, MI: Baker Books, 1994.

Harkin, Joy. ***Freedom: A History of Us.*** Oxford: Oxford University Press, 2003.

Hart, Benjamin. ***Faith and Freedom.*** Dallas: Lewis and Stanley Publishers, 1988.

Hicks, Laurel, editor. ***The Modern Age.*** Pensacola, FL: A Beka Book Publishing, 1981.

Hiscox, Edward T. ***The New Directory for Baptist Churches.*** Chicago: Judson Press, 1894.

Horton, Ronald. ***British Literature.*** Pensacola, FL: A Beka Publishing, 1993.

Huberman, Leo. *We the People.* New York: Monthly Review Press, 1940.

Irving, Washington. *Life and Voyages of Christopher Columbus, Vol. 1-2.* New York: P. F. Collier and Son, 1868.

Jehle, Paul. *Puritans and Witches.* San Antonio: Vision Forum, 2001.

Jennings, Gary. *Aztec.* New York: Atheneum, 1980.

Lampe, Craig. *The Forbidden Book.* Phoenix, AZ (No publisher given), 2003.

Linton, Calvin, editor. *The Bicentennial Almanac.* Nashville: Thomas Nelson Publishers, 1975.

Locke, John. *An Essay Concerning Human Understanding.* Boston: Cummings and Hilliard and J. T. Buckingham, 1813.

Lossing, B. J. *Lives of the Signers of the Declaration of Independence.* New York: George Cooledge and Brother, 1848. Reprinted Aledo, TX: Wallbuilders, 1996.

Marshall, Peter and David Manuel. *The Light and the Glory.* Grand Rapids, MI: Fleming H. Revell, 1977.

Martin, William. ***With God on Our Side.*** New York: Broadway Books, 1996.

McCullough, David. ***1776.*** New York: Simon and Schuster, 2005.

McPherson, James and Alan Brinkley. ***Days of Destiny.*** New York: D. K. Publishing, 2001.

Miller, John C. ***Origins of the American Revolution.*** Boston: Little Brown and Company, 1943.

Morison, Samuel Eliot. ***Admiral of the Seas.*** New York: MJF Books, 1942.

Morison, Samuel Eliot. ***The Growth of the American Republic.*** New York: Oxford University Press, 1950.

Newman, A. H. ***A History of Baptist Churches in the United States.*** Philadelphia: American Baptist Publishing Society, 1898.

Olasky, Marvin. ***Fighting for Liberty and Virtue.*** Washington, D.C.: Regnery Publishing, 1995.

Royal, Robert. ***1492 and All That.*** Washington, D.C.: Ethics and Public Policy Center, 1992.

Rushdooney, Rousas J. ***American History to 1865.*** Audio Cassette Series.

Scheer, George and Hugh Rankin. ***Rebels and Redcoats.*** New York: Perigee Books, 1983.

Schlesinger, Arthur, Jr., editor. ***The Almanac of American History.*** New York: Perigee Books, 1983.

Singer, C. Gregg. ***The Theological Interpretation of American History.*** Phillipsburg, NJ: Presbyterian and Reformed Publishing, 1964.

Spivey, Larkin. ***Miracles of the American Revolution.*** Fairfax, VA: Allegiance Press, 2004.

Stiles, T. J. ***The American Revolution.*** New York: Berkley Publishing Group, 1999.

Tuchman, Barbara W. ***The First Salute.*** New York: Alfred A. Knopf, 1988.

Walton, Rees. ***One Nation Under God.*** Nashville: Thomas Nelson Publishing, 1987.

Weaver, Neal and James Combs. ***Our Biblical Baptist Heritage.*** Shreveport, LA: Eagle Publishing, 2004.

Whitney, David. ***American Presidents.*** New York: Prentice Hall Press, 1993.

Wilkins, J. Steven. ***America the First 350 Years.*** Forest, MS: Covenant Publishing, 1988.

Willison, George. ***Saints and Strangers.*** New York: Reynal and Hitchcock, 1945.

www.ingramcontent.com/pod-product-compliance
Lightning Source LLC
Chambersburg PA
CBHW070637050426
42451CB00008B/197